SPECTRUM®

Language Arts

Grade 1

Published by Spectrum®
an imprint of Carson-Dellosa Publishing LLC
Greensboro, NC

Spectrum®
An imprint of Carson-Dellosa Publishing LLC
P.O. Box 35665
Greensboro, NC 27425 USA

04-179167811

Table of Contents Grade 1

Table of Contents, continued

Chapter 1 Grammar
Lesson 1.1 Common and Proper Nouns

A **common noun** names a person, place, or thing.

> girl (person)   School (place)   pen (thing)

A **proper noun** names a special person, place, or thing. A proper noun starts with a capital letter.

> **D**ego goes to **D**avis **E**lementary.
>
> **A**bby has a dog named **M**ilo.
>
> When will you move to **T**exas?

Complete It

Finish each sentence below. Use a common noun from the box.

buddy	park	ball	bench

1. Today, Leo and I went to the _____ .

2. He is my _____ .

3. We played catch with my _____ .

4. We sat on a _____ to drink our juice.

Tip	The words **a, an** and **the** can help you find nouns.
	a swing **an** orange **the** moon

Lesson 1.1   Common and Proper Nouns

Identify It

Look at each word in the box. If it is a proper noun, write it under **Proper Nouns**. If it is a common noun, write it under **Common Nouns**.

man	teacher	book	Long's Toy Store
Ben	New York	Anna	farm

Proper Nouns   **Common Nouns**

_____   _____

_____   _____

_____   _____

_____   _____

Lesson 1.1   Common and Proper Nouns

Sam

Miles

Amina

Rewrite It

Rewrite each sentence. Use a capital letter for each proper noun.

1. jess will go to dalton library today.

_____

2. mrs. ling works at green valley hospital.

_____

3. ted made a left turn on main street.

_____

Try It

Make a list of three proper nouns from your life. You can use names of people you know. You can use places you visit. Make sure to start each one with a capital letter.

_____

_____

_____

Lesson 1.2 Verbs

Verbs are action words. They tell what happens in a sentence.

  Jamal **drops** the ball.   Mia **laughs** at the joke.   Tim **sets** the table.

Identify It

Underline the verb in each sentence.

1. Imani and Kate jump rope.

2. Imani counts.

3. Kate trips on the rope.

4. Imani helps her friend.

Try It

Write another sentence about Imani and Kate. Underline the verb you use.

_____

Lesson 1.2 Verbs

Rewrite It

Rewrite each sentence. Change each underlined verb to a new verb. Choose from the verbs in the box.

trims	sings	draws	
walks	swims	reads	bikes

1. Nico skates every Friday.

_____

2. Ava runs home from school.

_____

3. Tess dances in her room.

_____

4. Jon climbs the trees in his yard.

_____

Review

A **common noun** names a person, place, or thing.

baby   park   library   car

A **proper noun** names a special person, place, or thing. It starts with a capital letter.

Danny   **L**ena   **F**lorida   **B**axter **H**ospital

A **verb** can be an action word. It tells what happens in a sentence.

eat   swim   clap   paint

Putting It Together

Read the sentences. Look at each underlined word. Write **CN** for **common noun** or **PN** for **proper noun**.

1. _____ <u>Erik</u> likes to play baseball.

2. _____ He moved here from <u>Ohio</u>.

3. _____ His <u>brother</u> plays, too.

4. _____ Ty gave Erik his old <u>mitt</u>.

5. _____ They will go to a game at <u>Blick Stadium</u>.

Review

Circle the verb that completes each sentence.

1. Zack and Nora (dropped, gave) Aunt Kerry a treat.

2. They (lost, baked) muffins.

3. Zack (ate, drew) her a picture.

4. Nora (picked, threw) a bunch of flowers.

5. Aunt Kerry (sat, hugged) Zack and Nora.

6. They (rode, hopped) their bikes home.

Lesson 1.3   Pronouns

A **pronoun** is a word that can take the place of a noun.

Ella paints a picture.   **She** paints a picture.

Omar and I like to draw.   **We** like to draw.

The words **I, me, you, he, she, him, her, it, we, us, they,** and **them** are pronouns.

Match It

Draw a line to match each word or words on the left with a pronoun on the right.

Ann   he

the crayon   they

Ben   it

Mom and Dad   she

Try It

Write one sentence using a noun. Then, rewrite it using a pronoun.

_____

_____

Lesson 1.3   Pronouns

Complete It

Read the story. Fill in each blank. Use the pronouns in the box. Make sure to start each sentence with a capital.

my	I	them	they
he	me	she	it

I love to make art. _____ hang up all my paintings in

my room. Mom painted one wall with special paint.

_____ said I can draw right on the wall!

_____ little brothers like it, too.   draw

while I am at school. Mom said I should let_____ . Jake

drew a dinosaur for _____ . I think _____ is

pretty cool. _____ wants to be an artist, too!

Lesson 1.4 Adjectives

An **adjective** is a word that describes a noun. It tells more about a noun. Adjectives can answer the question **What kind?**

the **yellow** duck   the **hard** rock   the **shiny** penny

Identify It

Circle the adjective in each sentence. Make a line under the noun it tells about.

Example: Samir has brown eyes.

1. Jada picked the pink roses.

2. A tiny bee buzzed around the garden.

3. Meg planted the green sprouts.

4. She wiped off her dirty hands.

5. Lex looked up at the tall sunflower.

6. What a hot day!

Tip	More than one adjective can tell about a noun. **three pink** pigs the **shiny**, **red** berries the **soft**, **cozy** blanket

Lesson 1.4   Adjectives

Solve It

Circle the adjectives from the box in the word search.

red	old	spicy	green
hot	smooth	nice	sad

```
q   r   e   d   z   b   b
o   d   s   a   d   j   h
l   n   w   h   l   t   o
d   i   s   s   q   e   t
c   c   g   r   e   e   n
r   e   y   u   m   a   f
s   m   o   o   t   h   n
x   k   s   p   i   c   y
```

Lesson 1.5 Prepositions

A **preposition** can show location (where) or time (when). Prepostions link nouns to other words in the sentence. Some common prepositions are **to, from, in, on, behind, at, below, near, by, above, into, off,** and **with.**

Example: The book is **below** the shelf.

Identify It

Each sentence below has one preposition. Find and circle the prepositions.

1. Hal put his hat on his head.

2. It was cold in the cave!

3. Water dripped from the ceiling.

4. A rock fell near Hal's foot.

5. The cave was filled with bats!

6. At 4:00, the cave tour was done.

Lesson 1.5 Prepositions

Complete It

Use the words in the box to complete each item below.

1. Where is the fox? _____ a box

2. Where is the bear? _____ the boy

3. Where is the girl? _____ the covers

4. Where is the cat? _____ the dog

5. Where is the dog house? _____ the dog

Try It

Write two sentences that tell a mouse might hide. Use a preposition in each sentence.

1. _____

2. _____

Review

A **pronoun** is a word that can take the place of a noun. **I, me, you, he, she, him, her, it, we, us, they,** and **them** are pronouns.

An **adjective** is a word that describes a noun. It tells more about a noun.

the **striped** pants   the **red** car   a **cloudy** day

A **preposition** is a word that links a noun to other words in a sentence. Some prepositions are **in, on, at, under, with,** and **from.**

Putting It Together

Circle the pronoun to finish each sentence.

1. Sam and (I, they) went to a farm.

2. (He, Us) had never seen real horses before.

3. Sam fed (she, them) some apples.

4. The owner let (we, us) brush Star.

5. We even got to ride (her, they).

6. (Us, We) had a lot of fun!

7. (They, It) was a great day on the farm.

Review

Write an adjective to describe each noun. Remember to ask **What kind?** about each noun. The words in the box can give you some ideas. You can also use your own words.

shiny	pink	hot	new
old	furry	gray	stinky

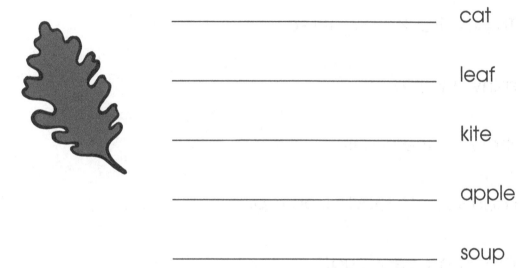

_____ cat

_____ leaf

_____ kite

_____ apple

_____ soup

Write a preposition to complete each sentence below.

1. Amad is_____ his swimming lesson.

2. Dad makes pancakes_____ Sunday mornings.

3. The salt is_____ the pepper.

4. Please take a jacket_____you!

Lesson 1.6   Sentences

A **sentence** is a complete thought. It starts with a capital letter. It ends with an end mark.

(T)im plays ball(.) (T)hat book is funny(.) (L)ook at the frog(.)

Identify It

Look at each group of words. If it is a sentence, make a check mark ✔ on the line. Circle the capital letter. Circle the end mark.

1. _____ The fire truck is bright red.

2. _____ shiny and clean

3. _____ shows us the hoses

4. _____ I can see the ladders on top.

5. _____ The siren is very loud.

6. _____ cover my ears

7. _____ We climb inside.

Lesson 1.6 Sentences

Rewrite It

Read each set of words below. Rewrite it as a sentence.
Make sure to start with a capital and end with a period.

1. our fire station has a dog

_____

2. he is white with black spots

_____

3. his name is Charlie

_____

4. he likes to ride in the truck

_____

Try It

Write two sentences about Charlie.

_____

_____

Lesson 1.7   Statements

A **statement** is a telling sentence. It starts with a capital letter. It ends with a period.

(A)nton is in first grade(.) (D)inner is ready(.)

Proof It

Read each statement below. If it does not start with a capital, make three lines under the letter (≡). Write the capital letter above. If the period is missing, add it and circle it.

E
ella lost her pencil(.)
≡

1. look outside on a clear, dark night.

2. You will see many stars

3. they are very far away

4. stars do not live forever.

5. Some groups of stars have names

6. our sun is a star

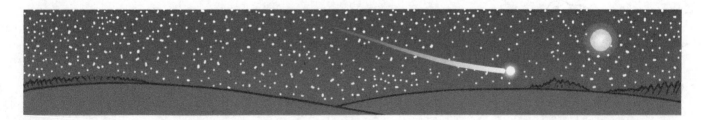

Lesson 1.7 Statements

Rewrite It

Rewrite the sentences. Each should begin with a capital and end with a period.

1. jaya has a telescope

_____

2. jaya likes to see the stars

_____

3. she can find the Big Dipper

_____

4. dad showed her Venus

_____

5. the moon is easy to spot

_____

Lesson 1.8   Questions

A **question** is an asking sentence. A question starts with a capital letter. It ends with a question mark.

(W)here is your house(?)   (W)hat time is i(?)   (D)o you have a ca(?)

Complete It

Complete each question with a question mark.

1. Who was the first U.S. president_____

2. Where was George Washington born _____

3. How long was he president_____

4. Did he live in the White House_____

5. What was Washington like as a boy_____

Try It

What if you could talk to George Washington? Write two questions you would ask him.

_____

_____

NAME _____

Match It

Read each statement about the White House. Read the questions in the box. Write the letter of the question that matches each statement.

A. How many rooms does it have?

B. Who was first to live in it?

C. How many chefs work there?

D. Who named the White House?

1. _____ Theodore Roosevelt named the White House.

2. _____ It has 132 rooms.

3. _____ Five chefs work at the White House.

4. _____ John Adams was first to live in it.

Tip Questions often begin with words like **who**, **what**, **where**, **when**, **how**, and **why**.

Lesson 1.9 Exclamations

An **exclamation** is a sentence that shows excitement. It can also show surprise. It starts with a capital letter. It ends with an exclamation point.

Ⓘ need help**!** Ⓦe won the game**!** Ⓥacation starts today**!**

Identify It

Read each pair of sentences. One sentence in each pair is a statement. The other sentence is an exclamation. Add the correct end marks.

1. I won the race _____

Today is Monday _____

2. Finn is my best friend _____

Finn found ten dollars _____

3. I have two sisters _____

Something is out there _____

Try It

What is something exciting in your life? Write an exclamation on the line.

_____

Lesson 1.9 Exclamations

Rewrite It

Rewrite each exclamation on the line. Remember, start with a capital. End with an exclamation point.

1. the dog got out

_____

2. don't knock over your cup

_____

3. lena's painting came in first place

_____

4. i lost my first tooth

_____

Tip	Some exclamations are just one word. **Help! Wow! Great! Ouch!**

Lesson 1.10 Combining Sentences

Sometimes, two sentences can be made into one. Both sentences must tell about the same thing.

Frogs live in the pond. Fish live in the pond.

Use the word **and** to join the parts of the sentence.

Frogs **and** fish live in the pond.

Complete It
Read the sentences.
Fill in the missing words.

1. Max went to the fair. Li went to the fair.

   Max _____ Li went to the fair.

2. Mom rode the Ferris wheel. Dad rode the Ferris wheel.

   _____and Dad rode the Ferris wheel.

3. The juice was cold. The ice cream was cold.

   The juice and_____were cold.

4. Li played two games. Mom played two games.

   _____ and Mom played two games.

Lesson 1.10 Combining Sentences

Identify It

Read the letter. Three pairs of sentences can be joined. Underline each pair.

June 12, 2014

Dear Ana,

Guess what? We went to the fair. I had fun. Marco had fun. We went on lots of rides. Tess stayed home. Jane stayed home. They are too little for the fair.

My ticket was lost. My money was lost. Don't worry, I was lucky. Marco found them. I left them in a bumper car. It was a great day. I love the fair.

Hope to see you soon!

Your friend,

Will

Review

A **sentence** is a complete thought. It starts with a capital. It ends with an end mark.

(It) is 4:00(.)

A **statement** is a telling sentence. It ends with a period.

(Mi)a loves cheese(.)

A **question** is an asking sentence. It ends with a question mark.

(Wh)ere are your shoes(?)

An **exclamation** shows excitement. It ends with an exclamation point.

(I) got stung by a bee(!)

Putting It Together

1. Look at the picture. Write a statement about it.

_____

2. Look at the picture. Write a question about it.

_____

3. Look at the picture. Write an exclamation about it.

_____

Review

Sometimes, two sentences can be joined. Use the word **and** to make two sentences into one.

Sara skates every week.   Kyle skates every week.

Sara **and** Kyle skate every week.

Rewrite each pair of sentences as one sentence.

1. Bears eat berries. Birds eat berries.

_____

2. Frogs like bugs. Toads like bugs.

_____

3. Cows graze on hay. Horses graze on hay.

_____

4. Mice eat acorns. Squirrels eat acorns.

_____

A sentence always begins with a capital letter. This shows that a new sentence is starting.

Ⓦhat is your name?   Ⓣasha has two birds.   Ⓘ see the train!

Proof It

Look for the words that should be capitalized. Mark the letter with three lines below it (≡). Then, write the capital above it.

Example:
     S
sonya will wear her red dress.
≡

bats are odd animals. They fly like birds. even so, they are not

birds. Bats are mammals, like dogs and cats. most bats eat bugs. some

eat fruit.

Bats sleep during the day. they are awake at night. They do not

see well. They make a very high sound. the sound bounces off things.

This tells bats where things are. it helps them get around.

Lesson 2.1 Capitalizing the First Word in a Sentence

Rewrite It

Rewrite each sentence. Make sure to begin with a capital letter.

1. last week, a bat got in our house.

_____

2. i didn't know what it was at first.

_____

3. mom caught it and let it go outside.

_____

4. that poor bat was scared!

_____

5. i don't think he'll be back.

_____

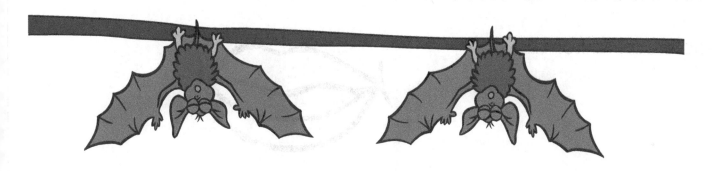

Lesson 2.2 Capitalizing the Pronoun I

The pronoun **I** is always capitalized. It can start a sentence. It can be in the middle of a sentence.

(**I**)ike pears.   (**I**)will wear a jacket.   Min and(**I**)want to swing.

Proof It

Read the story. Each time you see the word **I**, make sure it is capitalized. If it is not, make three lines below it (≡). Then, write the capital above it.

Example: Lulu and $\overset{\text{I}}{\underset{\equiv}{i}}$ went on a walk.

Last week, i went to the dentist. I was not nervous. i was just

getting a check-up. My sister had a tooth pulled once. Grace and

i were playing outside. She tripped and hit her mouth. I knew she

needed help, so i called for Mom. Mom and i took Grace right to Dr.

Cruz. i told him what happened. Then, Mom and I sat with Grace. She

was so brave! Her lip was puffy, but she was okay. Grace and i will be

more careful from now on!

Lesson 2.2   Capitalizing the Pronoun I

Try It

Read each sentence below. Write the word I in the box. Fill in the other blank with a word that finishes the sentence.

1. ☐ like to eat _____.

2. _____ and play catch.

3. ☐ like the color _____.

4. Each weekend, ☐ go _____.

5. My _____ and ☐ like to read books together.

6. ☐ have a cool _____.

Review

A sentence always begins with a capital letter.

(I)s that your train?   (L)et's plant the flowers.

The pronoun I is always spelled with a capital letter.

(I) forgot my lunch!   (L)ucy and I baked bread.

Look for the words that should be capitalized. Mark the letter with three lines below it (≡). Then, write the capital above it.

1. my best friend, Harry, has a fish tank.

2. harry and i went to the pet store.

3. he wanted to buy some fish food.

4. i like to look at all kinds of fish.

5. mom says my sister and i can get a small tank next year.

6. orange clownfish are the ones i like best.

Review

Rewrite each sentence. Make sure to use capitals where they are needed.

1. i have a new, red bike.

_____

2. my bike has a bell and a basket.

_____

3. ali and i ride to the library.

_____

Read each question. Answer it with a sentence that starts with **I**.

1. How old are you?

_____

2. What is your favorite food?

_____

3. What is one thing you like to do in the summer?

_____

Lesson 2.3 Capitalizing Names

Names begin with a capital letter. A person's name starts with a capital letter. A pet's name starts with a capital letter, too.

My sister's name is (E)mma.   I have a cat named (S)ocks.

Match It

The child and pet in each picture need a name. Choose a set of names from the box. Write them next to the picture. Make sure you start each name with a capital letter.

lily and lucky ben and bubbles	carlos and coco greg and gus	stella and star

_____ and _____

_____ and _____

_____ and _____

_____ and _____

_____ and _____

Lesson 2.3 Capitalizing Names

Proof It

The names below do not start with a capital letter. Find each letter that should be a capital letter. Make three lines below it (≡). Then, write the capital letter above it.

1. luke, jay, and Leo are all sam's brothers.

2. Lu named the kittens bella and sassy.

3. saw his friend ava at the park.

4. jess got to milk millie and Bonnie at the farm.

Try It

Write a sentence about two of your friends. Use their names in the sentence.

Lesson 2.4 Capitalizing Place Names

Place names begin with a capital letter.

Ⓓanville, Ⓚentucky   Ⓒove Ⓛibrary

Ⓜaple Ⓢtreet   Ⓙackson Ⓢchool

Ⓥenus   Ⓙapan

Proof It

The place names below do not start with a capital. Mark each letter that should be a capital with three lines below it (≡). Write the capital letter above it.

Example: We are going to m̲a̲ine this summer.
(with M written above, three lines under the m)

1. Ivan is moving to atlanta, georgia.

2. Do you think there is life on mars?

3. Addy goes to sandy brook elementary.

4. It snowed two feet in michigan!

5. Make a left turn on green road.

6. Lex swims at rock hill lake.

Lesson 2.4 Capitalizing Place Names

Try It

Answer each question. Make sure to start each place name with a capital letter.

I. What is the name of your street?

_____

2. What city were you born in?

_____

3. What is a state you would like to visit?

_____

4. What country do you live in?

_____

5. What is the name of a place you go a lot? It could be a school. Maybe it is a store or a library.

_____

Lesson 2.5 Capitalizing Days and Months

The **days of the week** start with a capital letter.

(M)onday, (T)uesday, (W)ednesday, (T)hursday, (F)riday, (S)aturday, Sunday

The **months of the year** start with a capital letter, too.

(J)anuary, (F)ebruary, (M)arch, (A)pril, (M)ay, (J)une, (J)uly,

(A)ugust, (S)eptember, (O)ctober, (N)ovember, (D)ecember

Solve It

Read each clue. Write the day of the week that matches it. Use the list above.

1. People like me a lot. I am the first day of the weekend.

   _____

2. I am the first weekday. My name starts with **m**. _____

3. You can find the word **sun** hiding in my name. _____

4. I am the last weekday. Here comes the weekend!

   _____

5. I come in the middle of the week. My name starts with **w**.

   _____

6. My name starts with **t**. I come near the end of the week.

   _____

7. My name starts with **t**, too. I come near the start of the week.

   _____

Lesson 2.5   Capitalizing Days and Months

Complete It

Fill in the month in each sentence. Make sure to use a capital letter.

1. (june)   Julia's birthday is in _____ .

2. (april)   Andy ate apples in _____ .

3. (july)   Jake plays jacks in _____ .

4. (may)   Mira met Matt in _____ .

5. (october)   Olly saw an owl in _____ .

6. (september)   Sam swam in _____ .

Try It

When is your birthday? _____

What is today's date? Ask an adult if you are not sure.

_____

Review

Names of people and pets start with a capital letter.

Give the book to (M)alik. Let's name the fish (B)uddy and (G)izmo.

Names of special places start with a capital letter, too.

(D)anville (H)ospital   (C)ap's (T)oy (S)tore

(C)hicago   (M)exico

Putting It Together

Complete each sentence with the word in the box. Make sure you begin names with a capital letter.

1. | lita | Rico and _____ were on vacation.

2. | cape cod | Their family was going

   to _____.

3. | sofia and joe | Cousins _____ were coming, too.

4. | tucker | _____, the poodle, rode on Mom's lap.

5. | dixie | The family cat, _____, stayed home.

6. | clean spoon diner | Dad stopped to get lunch at the

   _____.

Review

Days of the week start with a capital letter.

(T)uesday (S)aturday (W)ednesday

Months of the year start with a capital letter, too.

(M)arch (J)une (O)ctober

The days and months below do not start with a capital. Mark each letter that should be a capital with three lines below it (≡). Write the capital letter above it.

1. monday, march 8 is Eli's birthday.

2. Clare's dance is on saturday night.

3. It snowed on tuesday and wednesday.

4. My mom and dad were both born on december 2.

5. Kenji will be 7 on friday, april 20.

6. The store will open in september.

7. I saw a full moon on monday, july 11.

Lesson 2.6 Periods

A **period** is an end mark. It comes at the end of a sentence.

I have a hole in my pants. Luis has a loose tooth.

Complete It

Each sentence below is missing a period. Add it and circle it.

Example: Turn on the lights.

1. Giant pandas are found in China

2. They live in the mountains

3. There are not many pandas left in the wild

4. Pandas have black rings around their eyes

5. They can weigh 250 pounds

6. Pandas eat bamboo

7. They get most of their water from bamboo

Try It

Look at the picture of the panda above. Write a sentence about it. Make sure it ends with a period.

_____

Lesson 2.6 Periods

| Tip | A capital letter can show you where a new sentence start. |

Proof It

The periods are missing in the paragraph. Add them and circle them.

Baby pandas are called cubs A new baby is very small It is about the size of a stick of butter The cubs are not black and white They are pink A new cub looks more like a mouse than a bear It has almost no hair

A baby panda can not do much at first The baby's eyes stay shut for 6 to 8 weeks It takes a few months for a cub to learn to walk Baby pandas need their moms, just like baby humans

Lesson 2.7 Question Marks

A **question mark** comes at the end of a question. It shows where the question ends.

Can you play checkers**?** Where is my red bow**?** Have you seen Erin**?**

Rewrite It

Rewrite each question. Make sure it starts with a capital letter and ends with a question mark.

I. where are you moving

_____

2. have you packed yet

_____

3. who will drive the moving van

_____

4. what color is your new house

_____

5. how far away is it

_____

Lesson 2.7 Question Marks

Identify It

Read each pair of sentences. Add a period after each statement.
Add a question mark after each question. Underline the word that
tells you the sentence is a question.

1. What is your new address_____

   It is 811 Elm Street_____

2. I can't find my roller skates_____

   Have you seen them _____

3. What school do you go to_____

   I go to Shady Lane School _____

4. Nick and Izzy live next door_____

   Who lives in the blue house _____

5. Why are you moving _____

   My mom got a new job_____

Lesson 2.8 Exclamation Points

An **exclamation point** comes at the end of an exclamation. An exclamation is a sentence that shows excitement. It can also show surprise.

That's great news!   Look at the snake!   We won!

Identify It

Read each pair of sentences. Add a period after each statement. Add an exclamation point after each exclamation.

1. Today is Saturday_____

   It rained four inches today_____

2. Don't forget your umbrella_____

   Jon has a green umbrella _____

3. Watch out for that branch _____

   Dad will pick up the branches_____

4. Jaya did not step in the puddle _____

   My book fell in the puddle_____

Lesson 2.8 Exclamation Points

Try It

Look at each picture. Write an exclamation to go with it. Begin with a capital letter. End with an exclamation point.

_____

_____

_____

_____

Review

A statement ends with a **period.**

Aunt Kimm made pasta for dinner.

A question ends with a **question mark**.

How far away is Mars?

An exclamation ends with an **exclamation point**.

I smell smoke!

Putting It Together

Read each statement. Write a question to go with it. Be sure to end your question with a question mark.

Example: Question: What day is it?   Today is Monday.

1. Question:_____

Her name is Jazmin.

2. Question: _____

The book is on the desk.

3. Question:_____

I am six.

4. Question:_____

The ball is green.

Review

Read the letter. It is missing some end marks. Add three periods, three question marks, and two exclamation points.

Dear Owen,

How are you doing____ I am fine. Mom, Kate, and I

went on a picnic yesterday. Have you ever been to Falls

River Park____ It is beautiful____

We brought a blanket to sit on____ I spread it out.

Kate got the basket. Then, she sat down on the blanket.

Guess what happened____ She got stung by a bee!

Mom got the stinger out____ Kate did not even cry.

We ate our bread and cheese. We had some fruit

and cookies, too____ After we ate, we played catch.

What a fun picnic____

Your friend,

Noah

Lesson 2.9 Commas with Dates

A **comma** is a punctuation mark. In a date, it goes between the day and the year.

June 20, 1973   October 1, 2006   April 4, 1866

If a comma is missing, use this mark (∧) to add it.

March 17∧2014

Proof It

Commas are missing from the dates below. Use this mark (∧) to add them.

1. John moved to New York on December 23 1982.

2. Aunt Keiko was born on February 19 1979.

3. Grandma and Grandpa got married on May 6 1960.

4. I met Jada on July 11 2008.

5. Riley's birthday is August 14 2004.

Try It

When were you born? Write the date on the line. _____

Ask a friend when he or she was born. Write the date on the line.

_____

Lesson 2.9 Commas with Dates

Rewrite It

Rewrite each date. Use commas where they are needed.

1. January 5 1984 _____

2. November 18 2002 _____

3. May 23 1999 _____

4. February 9 2015 _____

5. July 31 1944 _____

6. September 12 1965 _____

7. April 29 1814 _____

Spectrum Language Arts
Grade 1

Lesson 2.10 Commas with Cities and States

A **comma** is used between the name of a city and state.

Detroit, Michigan   Wilmington, Delaware   Portland, Oregon

Proof It

Add a comma between each city and state. Use this mark (∧) to add each comma.

1. You may have heard of Chicago Illinois.

2. You might know Dallas Texas.

3. Have you heard of Chicken Alaska?

4. Would you like to go to Bumble Bee Arizona?

5. How about Two Egg Florida?

6. Is it boring to live in Boring Maryland?

7. What is it like in Moon Virginia?

Lesson 2.10 Commas with Cities and States

Complete It

Finish each sentence with a city and state from the box. Use commas where they are needed.

Lima Ohio	**Reneo Navada**	**Austin Texas**
Macon Georgia	**Portland Maine**	**Miami Florida**

1. Anton is moving to_____ .

2. In May, Izzy will go to _____ .

3. Lee's aunt lives in_____ .

4. It will take Cam two days to drive to _____ .

5. Dan found _____ on the map.

6. Jane has lived in _____ for 11 years.

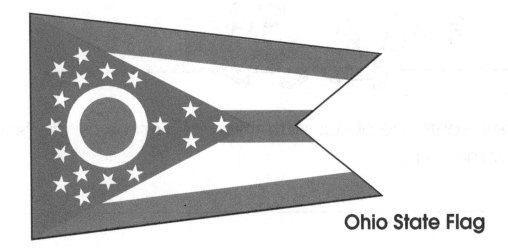

Ohio State Flag

Lesson 2.11 Apostrophes with Possessives

An **apostrophe plus s** (**'s**) shows that someone owns something.

Keisha**'s** book   Meg**'s** brush   Cody**'s** train

Complete It

Add **'s** to each blank below. Make a line under the item each person owns.

1. Emma_____drawing

2. Diego_____ pen

3. Mr. Stein_____truck

4. Dante_____ leaf

5. Kat_____frog

6. Jen _____ apple

Try It

Write a sentence about something a friend owns. Use **'s** to show what he or she owns.

_____

Lesson 2.11 Apostrophes with Possessives

Identify It

Read each pair of sentences. Make a check mark ✔ next to the one that is correct.

1. _____ Mia's hat

   _____ Mias hat

2. _____ Blakes bird'

   _____ Blake's bird

3. _____ Amad's boots

   _____ Amads boots

4. _____ Rosas muffin

   _____ Rosa's muffin

5. _____ Nicks snake'

   _____ Nick's snake

NAME _____

In a date, use a comma between the day and the month.

April 5, 1988   December 20, 2015   June 13, 2001

Use a comma between the name of a city and state.

St. Paul, Minnesota   Buffalo, New York   Nashville, Tennessee

Use this mark (∧) to add the missing commas.

1. My grandma was born on January 24 1936.

2. Chris sent a letter to Wichita Kansas.

3. How old will you be on January 1 2020?

4. A big snow storm hit Augusta Maine.

5. We stayed at a hotel in Madison Wisconsin.

6. The baby turned one on August 23 2009.

● Augusta

Review

An **apostrophe plus s** (**'s**) shows that someone owns something.

Manny**'s** house   Lily**'s** duck   Carter**'s** pail

Pick one word from Box 1 and one from Box 2. Write a possessive using your words.

Box 1	Tony	Zack	Dan
	Ella	Ming	Maria

Box 2	sock	sled	drum
	map	fish	doll

Example: Ming's doll

1. _____

2. _____

3. _____

4. _____

5. _____

6. _____

When a sentence is about one person or thing, add **s** to the verb.

<u>Jim</u> drop**s** the ball.   <u>The leaf</u> blow**s** away.

When a sentence is about more than one person or thing, do not add **s**.

<u>The cats</u> look for mice.   <u>Jeff and Yoko</u> play the piano.

Match It

Draw a line to match each sentence to the correct ending.

1. Ms. Ito   grades the tests.

                                                 grade the tests.

2. The pencils   fall on the floor.

                                                 falls on the floor.

3. The bell   ring at 3:00.

                                                 rings at 3:00.

4. The girls   paints in the art room.

                                                 paint in the art room.

5. Caleb   sings after school.

                                                 sing after school.

Lesson 3.1 Subject-Verb Agreement

Complete It

Circle the word that completes each sentence.

1. Max (puts, put) on his space suit.

2. He (slip, slips) on the boots.

3. The helmet (roll, rolls) across the floor.

4. Max and his dog (travel, travels) to outer space.

5. They (sees, see) Earth from far above.

6. Max's mom (calls, call) him home for dinner.

Lesson 3.2 Irregular Verbs: **Am, Is, Are**

The words **am**, **is**, and **are** are all verbs.

Use **am** with the word **I**.

I **am** happy.   I **am** cold.

Use **is** with one person or thing.

The balloon **is** red.   Seth **is** at the park.

Use **are** with more than one person or thing.

The pens **are** in my desk.   The boys **are** inside.

Rewrite It

Each sentence below has the wrong verb. Rewrite it with the correct verb. Choose from **is**, **am**, or **are**.

1. The farmer am ready to milk the cows.

   _____

2. I is glad to help Bill.

   _____

3. The horse are brown and white.

   _____

4. The kids is by the pond.

   _____

Lesson 3.2   Irregular Verbs: **Am**, **Is**, **Are**

Complete It

Complete each sentence with the correct word from the box. Write it on the line.

1. | **is**   **are** | The pig _____ in the mud.

2. | **am**   **are** | I _____ sure I let the dog out.

3. | **is**   **are** | The ducks _____ with their babies.

4. | **am**   **is** | The cow _____ next to the fence.

5. | **are**   **is** | Farmer Bill and Henry _____ in the kitchen.

6. | **is**   **are** | The pony _____ six months old.

Tip   Not all verbs are action verbs. **Am**, **is**, and **are** are not action verbs. Some other examples are **have**, **has**, was, and **were**.

Lesson 3.3   Past-Tense Verbs: **Was, Were**

The words **was** and **were** tell about something that happened in the past.

Use **was** with one person or thing.

> <u>The bike</u> **was** broken.   <u>I</u> **was** ready for dinner.

Use **were** with more than one person or thing.

> <u>Amit and Liza</u> **were** at the movies.   <u>The books</u> **were** in the car.

Proof It

Read each sentence. Check to see if the verbs **was** and **were** are correct. If you find a mistake, cross it out. Write the correct word above it.

                              was
Example: The worm ~~were~~ under the leaf.

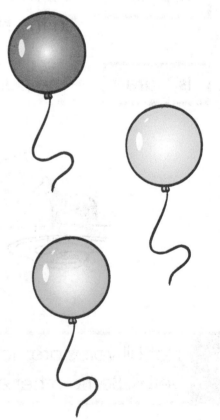

1. The parade were at 1:00.

2. The kids was excited to see it.

3. The balloons were red, yellow, and green.

4. The band were very loud.

5. Drew and Maggy was in the first float.

NAME _____

Lesson 3.3   Past-Tense Verbs: **Was, Were**

Complete It

Fill in each blank with **was** or **were.**

1. The drums_____ in the middle of the parade.

2. It _____ a sunny day.

3. We _____ lucky it didn't rain.

4. Mom and Dad_____ on the sidewalk.

5. Nico _____ the leader.

6. At the end of the parade, we _____tired!

Try It

Write a sentence telling how you felt on the first day of school. Use the verb **was** or **were**.

_____

Lesson 3.4   Past Tense: Add **ed**

Verbs in the **past tense tell** about things that already happened. Add **ed** to most verbs to tell about the past.

    It start**ed** to rain.   Henry knock**ed** on the door.

If a verb ends in **e**, just add **d.**

    live ⟶ lived   race ⟶ raced

Identify It

Circle the past-tense verb in each sentence.

1. The game started at 3:00.

2. A ball landed right next to me!

3. I picked it up.

4. The crowd cheered.

5. The game ended with a score of 4 to 3.

Try It

Write a sentence about something that happened last year. Use a verb that ends with **ed**.

_____

Lesson 3.4 Past Tense: Add **ed**

Complete It

Complete each sentence with the verb in the box. Add **d** or **ed** to put it in the past tense.

1. | look | The pitcher _____ at the batter.

2. | wait | We _____ to see the hit.

3. | race | The player _____ to first base.

4. | jump | Number 3 _____ up to catch the ball.

5. | sail | The ball _____ over the fence.

6. | smile | I _____ at my brother.

7. | want | We_____ to see a great game, and we did!

Review

When a sentence is about one person or thing, add **s** to the verb.

Aunt Lola cut(s) my hair.

When a sentence is about more than one person or thing,

do not add **s**.

The bears look for berries.

Use the verb **am** with the word **I**.   I **am** hiding.

Use the verbs **is** and **was** with one person or thing.

The pear **is** green.   Mr. Otis **was** sick today.

Use the verbs **are** or **were** with more than one person or thing.

The balls **are** in the gym.   The girls **were** smiling.

Putting It Together

Circle the word that completes each sentence.

1. The storm (is, are) getting closer.

2. I (am, is) not afraid of thunder.

3. The lights (blinks, blink) on and off.

4. Dad (light, lights) some candles.

5. My sisters and I (feel, feels) so cozy.

6. Once, we (was, were) without power for three days!

Review

Add **ed** to most verbs to tell about the past.

Ari kick**ed** the ball.

If a verb ends in **e**, just add **d**.

bake —→ baked

All the verbs in **bold** should be in the past tense. Cross them out. Write the correct verb above them.

1. It **snow** all night.

2. Eva and I **look** out the window.

3. We **climb** to the top of the hill.

4. We **skate** on the pond.

5. Mom **cook** hot soup for lunch.

6. I **hope** it would snow again!

Lesson 3.5 Contractions with **Not**

A **contraction** is a way to join two words together. It is a shorter way to say something. An apostrophe (') takes the place of the missing letters.

Here are some contractions with **not**.

is not = isn't   are not = aren't

was not = wasn't   were not = weren't

does not = doesn't   did not = didn't

have not = haven't   can not = can't

Identify It

Read each sentence below. On the line, write a contraction for the underlined words.

1. I <u>can not</u> wait to go bowling. _____

2. I <u>have not</u> ever gone before. _____

3. Mom said <u>it is not</u> easy to knock over all the pins. _____

4. It <u>was not</u> hard to pick a ball. _____

5. There <u>were not</u> too many that fit my hand. _____

6. We <u>are not</u> going to be home by bedtime! _____

Lesson 3.5   Contractions with **Not**

Match it

Draw a line to match each pair of words to its contraction.

Lesson 3.6   Plurals with **s**

Plural means **more than one**. To make most nouns plural, just add **s**.

one hand → two hands   one plane → four planes

one tent → six tents   one hen → twelve hens

Solve It

Write the plural of each word on the line.
Then, circle the plurals in the puzzle.

bug ———————————   spider ———————————

beetle ———————————   cricket ———————————

wasp ———————————   ant ———————————

e	q	c	b	u	g	s
z	a	r	f	b	j	l
s	p	i	d	e	r	s
w	m	c	q	e	x	p
d	m	k	p	t	k	p
i	y	e	v	l	g	g
a	n	t	s	e	o	d
w	a	s	p	s	n	u

Lesson 3.6 Plurals with **s**

Complete It

Add an **s** to each noun to make it plural.

1. Sanj found three ladybug_____ .

2. Draw that moth with your marker_____ .

3. Did you see the bee _____fly back to their hive?

4. Jose saw four slug_____ in the garden.

5. Our dog _____get fleas every summer.

6. Watch out for tick _____in the woods!

7. Five inchworm_____ crawled up the leaf.

Lesson 3.7   Irregular Plural Nouns

For some words, do not add s to make the plural. Instead, the whole word changes.

One	More Than One
goose	geese
man	men
woman	women
tooth	teeth
child	children
mouse	mice
foot	feet

Other words do not change at all. Use the same word for one and more than one.

one deer → five deer   one fish → ten fish

one sheep → three sheep   one moose → eight moose

Look at each picture. Circle the word that names the picture.

deers deer	feet foot
woman women	children child
gooses geese	moose mooses

NAME ______________________________

Lesson 3.7 Irregular Plural Nouns

Solve It

Look at each number and picture below. Fill in the missing word on the line. Choose from the words in the box.

mouse	**men**	**fish**
sheep	**mice**	**teeth**

4 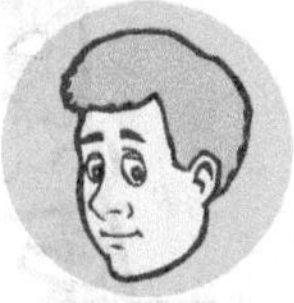 ______________________

6 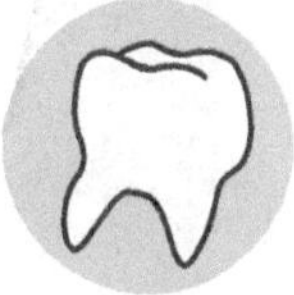 ______________________

1 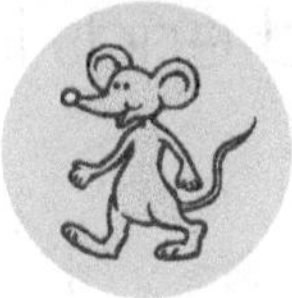 ______________________

50 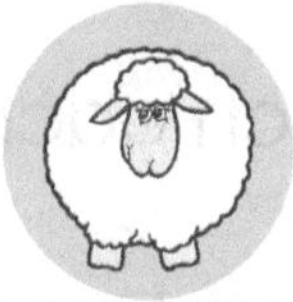 ______________________

17 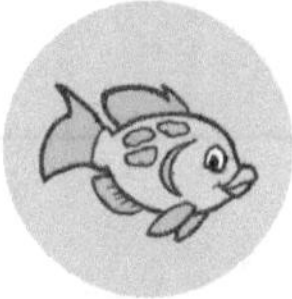 ______________________

22 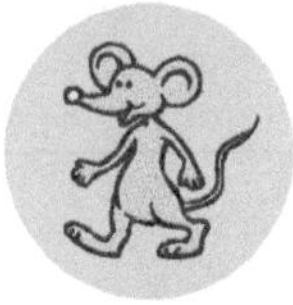 ______________________

Lesson 3.8   Prefixes and Suffixes

A **prefix** is added to the beginning of a root word. It changes the word's meaning.

The prefix **un** means **not** or **opposite of**.
Example: **un**healthy = **not** healthy

The prefix **re** means **again**.
Example: **re**wash = wash **again**

A **suffix** is added to the end of a root word.
It changes the word's meaning.

The suffix **er** means **one who.**
Example: bake**r** = one who bakes

The suffix **ed** means that something
happened **in the past**. (Remember, if a word ends in **e**, just add **d**).

Example: <u>Yesterday</u>, Luis wash**ed** the dog.

Match It

On the line, write a word with a suffix to match each meaning.

1. read again= _____

2. opposite of dress= _____

3. not sure= _____

4. copy again= _____

5. told again= _____

6. not able= _____

7. fill again= _____

Lesson 3.8 Prefixes and Suffixes

Complete It

Each **bold** word is missing a suffix. Add the suffix **er** or **ed**. Use the meaning of the sentence to decide which one to add.

1. Riley wants to be a **paint**_____one day.

2. Kris **smile**_____ at the baby.

3. Lena **tuck**_____her doll into bed.

4. The **catch**_____stands behind home plate.

5. Mom handed a check to the **bank**_____.

Sort the words in the box. Write them under the correct headings.

reuse	**liked**	**unhurt**	**farmer**
singer	**resell**	**fixed**	**unfair**

Words with Prefixes   Words with Suffixes

_____   _____

_____   _____

_____   _____

_____   _____

Review

A **contraction** is a way to join two words together. An apostrophe (') takes the place of the missing letters.

is not = isn't   are not = aren't   was not = wasn't

Putting It Together
Read each pair of words. Write a sentence using a contraction for those words.

I. is not _____ .

2. did not _____ .

3. was not _____ .

A **prefix** is added to the beginning of a root word. A **suffix** is added to the end of root word. Prefixes and suffixes change a word's meaning.

un = **not** or **opposite of**   **re** = **again**
er = **one who**   **ed** = **in the past**

Circle a prefix and a suffix in each item.

I. Did the baker reheat the pizza?

2. Tia was unhappy that the play lasted so long.

3. The builder sanded all the wood.

4. Mac skated to the bench to untie his laces.

Review

Plural means **more than one**. To make most nouns plural, just add **s**.

stamp → stamp(s)   cat → ca(ts)

For some words, do not add **s** to make the plural. Instead, the whole word changes.

foot → feet   woman → women

Other words do not change at all. Use the same word for one and more than one.

one sheep → four sheep   one moose → six moose

Look at each word. Write the plural on the matching sock.

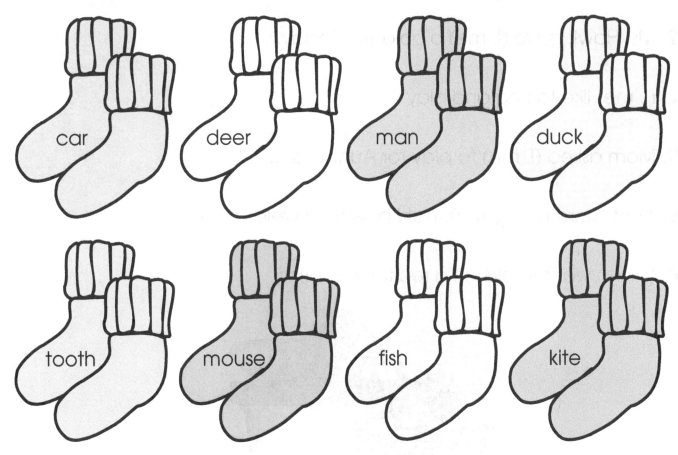

car   deer   man   duck

tooth   mouse   fish   kite

Lesson 3.9 Pronouns **I** and **Me**

You use the words **I** and **me** to talk about yourself.

   I like bananas.   Amit gave **me** a new book.

When you talk about yourself and another person, put them first.

   Devon and I ride the bus.   Eli made dinner for **Dad and me**.

Identify It

Circle **I** or **me** for each sentence.

1. (I, me) take piano lessons on Tuesdays.

2. Ms. Hawk gave (I, me) a gold star today.

3. (I, me) like to sing and play.

4. Mom asked (I, me) to play for Aunt Clare.

5. Aunt Clare told (I, me) that I play very well.

6. (I, me) want to play in a recital this spring.

Lesson 3.9 Pronouns **I** and **Me**

Complete It

Read the story. Write **I** or **me** in each blank to complete
the sentences.

_____ play the violin. My grandma gave _____ one. It was

hers. _____ have a picture of her playing it. She told _____ to

practice every day.

My friend Avi and _____ take lessons. I started when _____

was three. He and _____ like to play together. He told _____ he

wants to play the piano, too. My grandma says she can teach Avi

and _____.

Lesson 3.10 Comparative Adjectives

Some adjectives are used to compare. Add **er** to an adjective to compare two things. Add **est** to compare three or more things.

Joe's dog is small.

Tasha's dog is small**er**.

Anton's dog is small**est**.

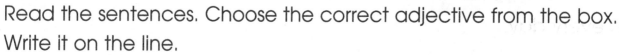

Identify It

Read the sentences. Choose the correct adjective from the box. Write it on the line.

1. | oldest older | Sami is the _____ of all her sisters.

2. | softer softest | Lola's pillow is _____ than mine.

3. | louder loudest | My alarm clock is _____ than yours.

4. | shorter shortest | Max has the _____ hair of all.

5. | slow slowest | Kiku's turtle is _____ than Alex's turtle.

Try It

Write two sentences. Compare two things in each sentence. Us these adjectives or one of your own: **harder, fastest, coldest, darker, youngest, longer**.

1. _____

2. _____

Lesson 3.10 Comparative Adjectives

Complete It

Fill in the yellow spaces below with the correct adjective.

	newer	newest
warm	warmer	
hard		hardest
neat	neater	
	smarter	smartest
tall		tallest

Review

You use the words **I** and **me** to talk about yourself.

I can make eggs.   The blue jay saw **me**.

When you talk about yourself and another person, put them first.

Grandpa and I play chess.   Give the books to **Chen and me**.

Putting It Together

Read each pair of sentences. Make a check mark ✔ next to the one that is correct.

1. _____ Me have a baby sister.

   _____ I have a baby sister.

2. _____ She gives me sloppy kisses.

   _____ She gives I sloppy kisses.

3. _____ Birdy and I play hide and seek.

   _____ Me and Birdy play hide and seek.

4. _____ She likes to chase I, too.

   _____ She likes to chase me, too.

Review: Chapter 3 Lessons 9–10
Usage

Review

Some adjectives are used to compare. Add **er** to an adjective to compare two things. Add **est** to compare three or more things.

Mick's room is neat.

A.J.'s room is neat**er**.

Izzy's room is neat**est**.

Fill in the blanks in each set of sentences.

1. Duke is a smart dog.

Bo is _____ than Duke.

Daisy is the_____ of all three dogs.

2. My house is old.

Lena's house is _____than mine.

Olly's house is the _____.

3. The yellow fish is small.

The green fish is _____.

The orange fish is the _____.

Lesson 3.11 Synonyms

Synonyms are words that mean the same or almost the same thing.

little, small   choose, pick   dad, father

Match It

Read each word. Find its synonym in the box. Write it in the matching mitten.

jump	sleepy	glad
fast	shout	large

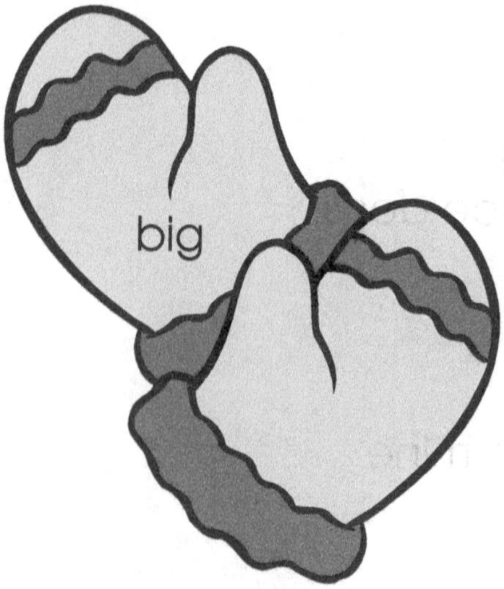

big

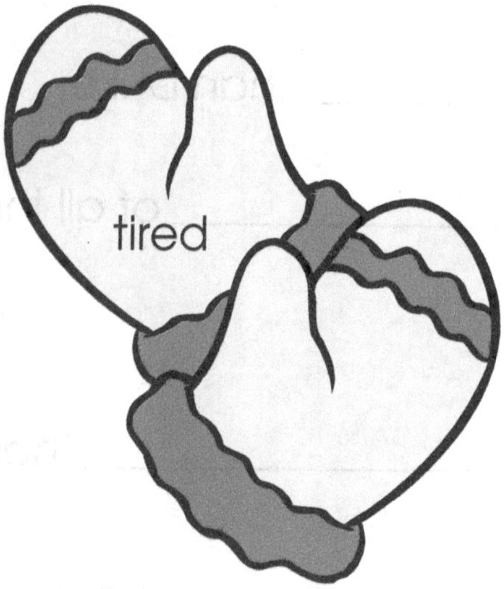

tired

quick

hop

happy

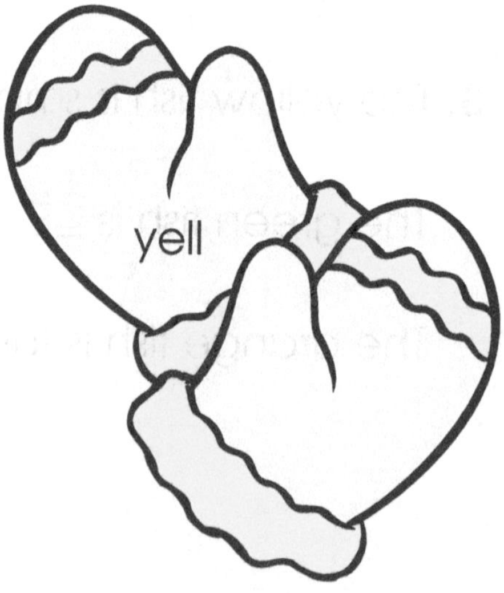

yell

Lesson 3.11 Synonyms

Complete It

Read each sentence. Find a synonym in the box for the underlined word. Write the synonym on the line.

toss	ship	small
begin	laughs	mother

1. Please <u>throw</u> me that ball. _____

2. My <u>mom</u> made waffles this morning. _____

3. Don't <u>start</u> the movie without me. _____

4. Luke has a <u>little</u> dog. _____

5. The <u>boat</u> is white and blue. _____

6. Devi <u>giggles</u> at my jokes. _____

Lesson 3.12   Antonyms

Antonyms are words that are opposites.

hot, cold   black, white   old, young

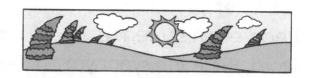

Complete It

Fill in each blank with a word from the box.

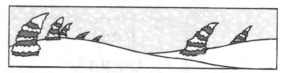

sad	front	go
night	down	full

1. The opposite of **day** ☼ is _____.

2. The opposite of **empty** 🥛 is _____.

3. The opposite of **happy** 🙂 is _____.

4. The opposite of **up** ⬆ is _____.

5. The opposite of **stop** STOP is _____.

6. The opposite of **back** is _____.

Lesson 3.12 Antonyms

Match It

Draw a line to match each word to its antonym.

right	last
first	tiny
new	loud
win	wrong
huge	out
in	old
quiet	lose

Try It

Draw a picture of two things that are opposites.

Lesson 3.13 Homophones

Homophones are words that sound the same. They have different spellings. They have different meanings, too.

to = toward	Throw it **to** me.
two = the number **2**	Nell has **two** cats.
too = also or very	Saki will come, **too**.
won = past tense of **win**	The Bears **won** the game!
one = the number **I**	**One** frog hopped away.
right = the opposite of left	Raise your **right** hand.
write = to put words on paper	Can you **write** your name?

Identify It

Underline the correct word to complete each sentence.

1. Jake bakes (won, one) cake.

2. Liam bakes (too, two) loaves of bread.

3. Reese can (write, right) down the recipes.

4. The flour is on the shelf on your (write, right).

5. Bella (won, one) first place in the bake-off!

Lesson 3.13 Homophones

Proof It

Make a line through each incorrect homophone. Write the correct word above it.

1. Carter will bring the muffins two school.

2. Set up too tables for the bake sale.

3. Right down the names of all the pies.

4. Only won loaf of bread is left!

Try It

1. Write a sentence using the word **write**.

_____

2. Write a sentence using the word **two**.

_____

Lesson 3.14 Multiple-Meaning Words

Some words are spelled the same but have different meanings.

Pat caught a **cold** last week.   **cold** = an illness

It is **cold** outside.   **cold** = chilly; not warm

Match It

Read each sentence. Think about how the word in **bold** is used.
Draw a line to the picture that shows it.

1. Ivan swung the **bat.**

2. The **bat** looked for some bugs
   to eat for dinner.

3. Maddy can tell time
   on her new **watch.**

4. **Watch** the birds in the tree.

Lesson 3.14 Multiple-Meaning Words

Try It

Read each pair of sentences. Look at the meaning of the first word in **bold**.
Then, write the word's other meaning.

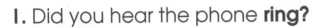

1. Did you hear the phone **ring?**

   ring: the sound a phone makes

   Kelly tried on Mom's wedding **ring.**

   ring: _____

2. **Park** the car across the street.

   park: to drive a car into a space

   There are new swings at the **park.**

   park: _____

3. We **saw** Ruby at the store.

   saw: watched or looked at

   Use the **saw** to cut the log.

   saw: _____

Review

Synonyms are words that mean the same thing.

    glad, happy   jump, hop   close, near

Antonyms are words that are opposites.

    push, pull   yes, no   hard, soft

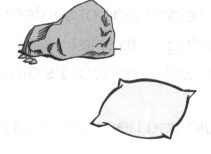

Putting It Together

Read each pair of words. If they are **antonyms**, write **A** on the line. If they are **synonyms**, write **S**.

1. _____ friend, buddy

2. _____ tight, loose

3. _____ right, wrong

4. _____ quick, fast

5. _____ day, night

6. _____ tired, sleepy

7. _____ love, hate

Write one sentence that has a pair of antonyms.

Example: Are you hot or cold?

_____

Homophones are words that sound the same. They have different spellings. They have different meanings, too.

to = toward   **two** = the number **2**   **too** = also or very

won = past tense of **win**   **one** = the number **I**

right = the opposite of **left**   **write** = to put words on paper

Write the word from the box that completes each sentence.

1.  Nate turned _____ at the stop sign.

2. | Two | Too |

   _____ kids were at the front of the group.

3. | to | two |

   Ms. Dugg gave some water _____ us.

4. 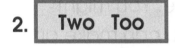 Only _____ person can come in first.

NAME _____

Before you write, you need a plan. Start with a list of ideas. You may not use all of them. Still, you will find one or two great ideas.

Sit down with a pen and piece of paper. Make a list. What are some things you know about? What would you like to learn more about?

karate	trains
dolphins	rabbits
being a doctor	soccer

Once you pick your topic, you may need to learn more. You might look in a book. You can also use the Internet. Then, you can make an idea web. This puts your ideas in order.

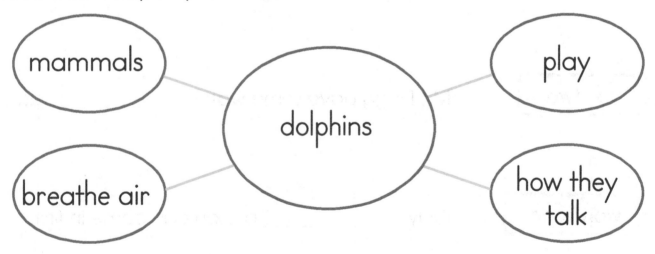

Try It

On a sheet of paper, make your own list of ideas. Which one do you like best? Make an idea web with the one you picked.

Lesson 4.2 Writer's Guide: Writing

The next step is to start writing. Use your idea web to help you. Do not worry too much about mistakes. This is just a rough draft. You can edit your work later.

Dolphins

Dolphins are intresting animals. They look like fish. they are really mammals. Whales are mammals too. This means they have warm blood They also need to breathe air. They use a blowhole to breathe.

Dolphins like two play. They are also very smart They talk to each other with clicks and whistles. humans know a lot about dolphins.

Try It

Write a rough draft on another piece of paper. Use your idea web to help you get started.

Lesson 4.3 Writer's Guide: Revising

Now it is time to **revise**. Read your work again. You can even read it out loud. Look for:

- words or sentences that don't belong.
- places you need more information.

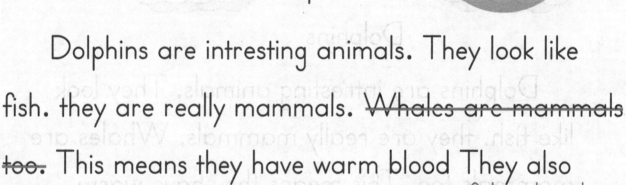

Dolphins

Dolphins are intresting animals. They look like fish. they are really mammals. ~~Whales are mammals too.~~ This means they have warm blood They also
on top of their head
need to breathe air. They use a blowhole∧to breathe.

Dolphins like two play. They are also very smart.
They talk to each other with clicks and whistles.
H   We still have a lot to learn.
humans know a lot about dolphins.∧
=

Try It

Look at the rough draft you wrote. How can you make it better? Mark your changes. If you need to, make a new copy of your writing.

Lesson 4.4　Writer's Guide: Proofreading

The next step is to look for mistakes. This is called **proofreading.**
Ask yourself:

- Does each sentence start with a capital letter?
- Does each sentence end with a punctuation mark?
- Are all the words spelled correctly?

Proofreading Marks

∧ = add	Cal is seven y^aers old.
⊙ = add a period	Saki has a blue hat⊙
≡ = make a letter a capital	Mr. hale lives next door.

Dolphins

Dolphins are int^eresting animals. They look like fish. they are really mammals. This means they have warm blood⊙They also need to breathe air. They use a blowhole on top of their head to breathe.

Dolphins like ~~two~~ to play. They are also very smart⊙ They talk to each other with clicks and whistles.

Humans know a lot about dolphins. We still have a lot to learn.

Try It

Proofread your writing. Use the marks you have learned.

Lesson 4.5   Writer's Guide: Publishing

Make the changes you marked. Then, make a final, neat copy of your work. You are ready to publish! **Publishing** means sharing your work. There are lots of ways to share writing.

- **Read your writing out loud.** Ask your friends, family, or class to listen.
- Make a copy of your work. **Mail it** to someone you know.
- Read your work out loud. Ask a parent or teacher to **make a video** of it.

- Have an adult help you **put your work in an e-mail**. You can send it to family and friends.

Try It

Choose one of the ideas above. What did your friends and family say? What are some others ways to share your writing?

Lesson 4.6 Writer's Guide: Writing a Friendly Letter

Start with **Dear** and the person's name, and a comma. Use capital letters.

June 16, 2011

Write the date in the right corner.

Dear Aunt Jen,

Last week, we went to the beach. Dad and I went fishing. Guess what we saw? Three dolphins were playing! They jumped and splashed. It looked like they were smiling.

Dad and I did not catch many fish. That's okay. The dolphins were the best part of the day.

I hope you can visit soon. I miss you. Say hi to Uncle Nate.

Love,

Blake

The body of a letter is a place to share news.

A closing can be words like **Love**, **Yours Truly**, or **Your Friend**. A closing starts with a capital. Add a comma after the closing.

Sign your name. Remember to start it with a capital.

Try It

Write a letter to someone you know. Make sure to check for mistakes. Ask an adult to help you mail it. Maybe you will get a letter back!

Chapter I Grammar
Lesson I.I Common and Proper Nouns

A **common noun** names a person, place, or thing.

girl (person)   School (place)   pen (thing)

A **proper noun** names a special person, place, or thing. A proper noun starts with a capital letter.

Diego goes to Davis Elementary.
Abby has a dog named Milo.
When will you move to Texas?

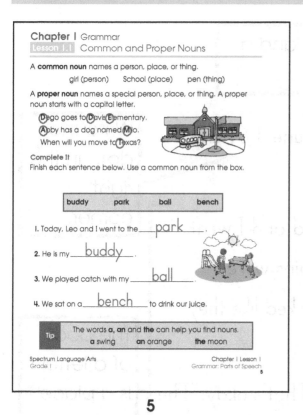

Complete It
Finish each sentence below. Use a common noun from the box.

buddy	park	ball	bench

I. Today, Leo and I went to the ___park___

2. He is my ___buddy___

3. We played catch with my ___ball___

4. We sat on a ___bench___ to drink our juice.

Tip	The words **a, an** and **the** can help you find nouns. a swing an orange the moon

Spectrum Language Arts
Grade I

Chapter I Lesson I
Grammar: Parts of Speech
5

5

Lesson I.I Common and Proper Nouns

Identify It
Look at each word in the box. If it is a proper noun, write it under **Proper Nouns**. If it is a common noun, write it under **Common Nouns**.

man	teacher	book	Long's Toy Store
Ben	New York	Anna	farm

Proper Nouns	Common Nouns
Ben	Man
New York	book
Anna	teacher
Long's Toy Store	farm

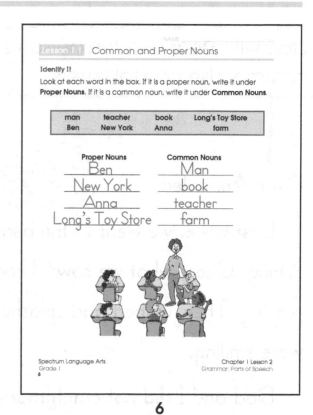

Spectrum Language Arts
Grade I

Chapter I Lesson 2
Grammar: Parts of Speech
6

6

Lesson I.I Common and Proper Nouns

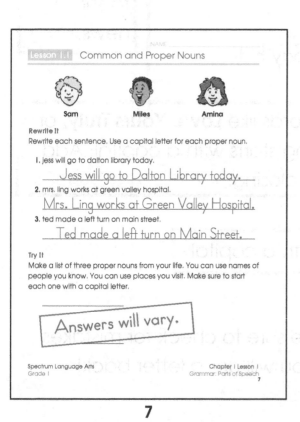

Sam   Miles   Amina

Rewrite It
Rewrite each sentence. Use a capital letter for each proper noun.

I. jess will go to dalton library today.
___Jess will go to Dalton Library today.___

2. mrs. ling works at green valley hospital.
___Mrs. Ling works at Green Valley Hospital.___

3. ted made a left turn on main street.
___Ted made a left turn on Main Street.___

Try It
Make a list of three proper nouns from your life. You can use names of people you know. You can use places you visit. Make sure to start each one with a capital letter.

___Answers will vary.___

Spectrum Language Arts
Grade I

Chapter I Lesson I
Grammar: Parts of Speech
7

7

Lesson I.2 Verbs

Verbs are action words. They tell what happens in a sentence.

Jamal **drops** the ball.   Mia **laughs** at the joke.   Tim **sets** the table.

Identify It
Underline the verb in each sentence.

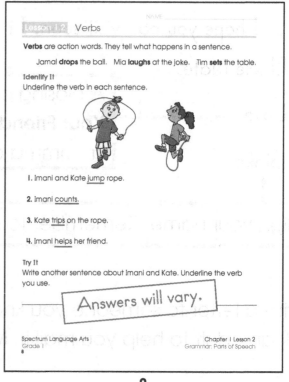

I. Imani and Kate <u>jump</u> rope.

2. Imani <u>counts</u>.

3. Kate <u>trips</u> on the rope.

4. Imani <u>helps</u> her friend.

Try It
Write another sentence about Imani and Kate. Underline the verb you use.

___Answers will vary.___

Spectrum Language Arts
Grade I

Chapter I Lesson 2
Grammar: Parts of Speech
8

8

Lesson 1.2 Verbs

Rewrite It
Rewrite each sentence. Change each underlined verb to a new verb. Choose from the verbs in the box.

trims	sings	draws	bikes
walks	swims	reads	

Answers will vary. Possible answers:

1. Nico skates every Friday.
   Nico swims every Friday.

2. Ava runs home from school.
   Ava walks home from school.

3. Tess dances in her room.
   Tess sings in her room.

4. Jon climbs the trees in his yard.
   Jon trims the trees in his yard.

Spectrum Language Arts
Grade 1

Chapter 1 Lesson 2
Grammar: Parts of Speech
9

Review

A **common noun** names a person, place, or thing.

| baby | park | library | car |

A **proper noun** names a special person, place, or thing. It starts with a capital letter.

| Danny | Lena | Florida | Baxter Hospital |

A **verb** can be an action word. It tells what happens in a sentence.

| eat | swim | clap | paint |

Putting It Together
Read the sentences. Look at each underlined word. Write **CN** for **common noun** or **PN** for **proper noun**.

1. PN Erik likes to play baseball.

2. PN He moved here from Ohio.

3. CN His brother plays, too.

4. CN Ty gave Erik his old mitt.

5. PN They will go to a game at Blick Stadium.

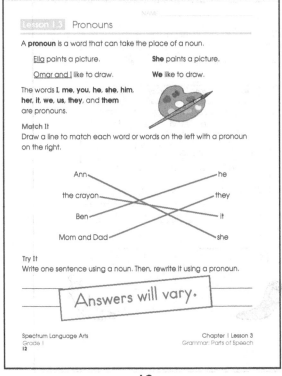

Spectrum Language Arts
Grade 1
10

Review: Chapter 1 Lessons 1-2
Grammar: Parts of Speech

Review

Circle the verb that completes each sentence.

1. Zack and Nora (dropped, (gave)) Aunt Kerry a treat.

2. They (lost, (baked)) muffins.

3. Zack (ate, (drew)) her a picture.

4. Nora ((picked), threw) a bunch of flowers.

5. Aunt Kerry (sat, (hugged)) Zack and Nora.

6. They ((rode), hopped) their bikes home.

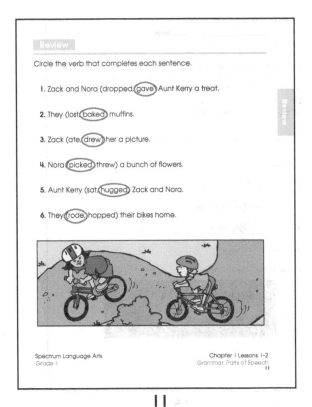

Spectrum Language Arts
Grade 1

Chapter 1 Lessons 1-2
Grammar: Parts of Speech
11

Lesson 1.3 Pronouns

A **pronoun** is a word that can take the place of a noun.

Ella paints a picture.   **She** paints a picture.

Omar and I like to draw.   **We** like to draw.

The words **I, me, you, he, she, him, her, it, we, us, they,** and **them** are pronouns.

Match It
Draw a line to match each word or words on the left with a pronoun on the right.

Ann ——————— he

the crayon ——— they

Ben —————— it

Mom and Dad ——— she

Try It
Write one sentence using a noun. Then, rewrite it using a pronoun.

Answers will vary.

Spectrum Language Arts
Grade 1
12

Chapter 1 Lesson 3
Grammar: Parts of Speech

13

Complete It

Read the story. Fill in each blank. Use the pronouns in the box. Make sure to start each sentence with a capital.

my	I	them	they
he	me	she	it

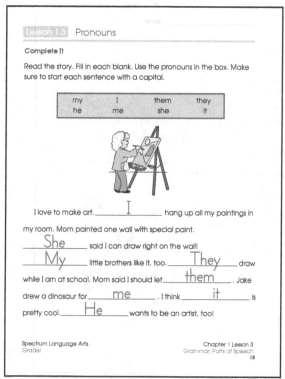

I love to make art. ___I___ hang up all my paintings in my room. Mom painted one wall with special paint.

___She___ said I can draw right on the wall!

___My___ little brothers like it, too. ___They___ draw while I am at school. Mom said I should let ___them___. Jake drew a dinosaur for ___me___. I think ___it___ is pretty cool. ___He___ wants to be an artist, too!

Spectrum Language Arts
Grade 1
Chapter 1 Lesson 3
Grammar: Parts of Speech
13

14

An **adjective** is a word that describes a noun. It tells more about a noun. Adjectives can answer the question **What kind?**

the **yellow** duck   the **hard** rock   the **shiny** penny

Identify It
Circle the adjective in each sentence. Make a line under the noun it tells about.

Example: Samir has (brown) eyes.

1. Jada picked the (pink) roses.
2. A (tiny) bee buzzed around the garden.
3. Meg planted the (green) sprouts.
4. She wiped off her (dirty) hands.
5. Lex looked up at the (tall) sunflower.
6. What a (hot) day!

Tip	More than one adjective can tell about a noun. **three pink** pigs the **shiny, red** berries the **soft, cozy** blanket

Spectrum Language Arts
Grade 1
Chapter 1 Lesson 4
Grammar: Parts of Speech
14

15

Solve It

Circle the adjectives from the box in the word search.

red	old	spicy	green
hot	smooth	nice	sad

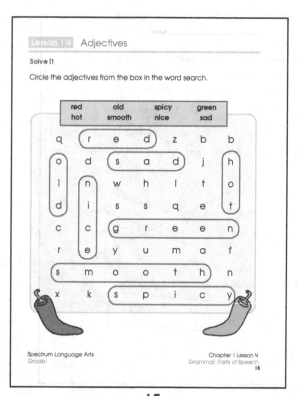

Spectrum Language Arts
Grade 1
Chapter 1 Lesson 4
Grammar: Parts of Speech
15

16

A **preposition** can show location (where) or time (when). Prepositions link nouns to other words in the sentence. Some common prepositions are **to, from, in, on, behind, at, below, near, by, above, into, off,** and **with.**

Example: The book is **below** the shelf.

Identify It
Each sentence below has one preposition. Find and circle the prepositions.

1. Hal put his hat (on) his head.
2. It was cold (in) the cave!
3. Water dripped (from) the ceiling.
4. A rock fell (near) Hal's foot.
5. The cave was filled (with) bats!
6. (At) 4:00, the cave tour was done.

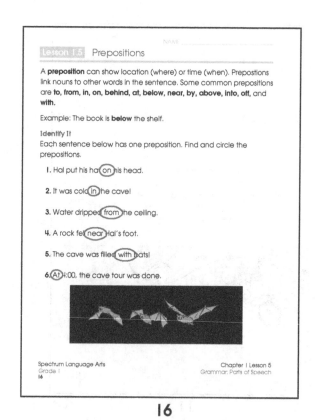

Spectrum Language Arts
Grade 1
Chapter 1 Lesson 5
Grammar: Parts of Speech
16

Lesson 1.5 Prepositions

Complete It
Use the words in the box to complete each item below.

1. Where is the fox? ____in____ a box

2. Where is the bear? ____beside____ the boy

3. Where is the girl? ____under____ the covers

4. Where is the cat? ____above____ the dog

5. Where is the dog house? ____behind____ the dog

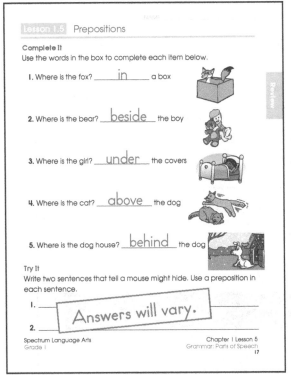

Try It
Write two sentences that tell a mouse might hide. Use a preposition in each sentence.

1. _____
Answers will vary.
2. _____

Spectrum Language Arts
Grade 1
Chapter 1 Lesson 5
Grammar: Parts of Speech
17

Review

A **pronoun** is a word that can take the place of a noun. **I, me, you, he, she, him, her, it, we, us, they,** and **them** are pronouns.

An **adjective** is a word that describes a noun. It tells more about a noun.

the **striped** pants   the **red** car   a **cloudy** day

A **preposition** is a word that links a noun to other words in a sentence. Some prepositions are **in, on, at, under, with,** and **from.**

Putting It Together
Circle the pronoun to finish each sentence.

1. Sam and (I, they) went to a farm.

2. (He, Us) had never seen real horses before.

3. Sam fed (she, them) some apples.

4. The owner let (we, us) brush Star.

5. We even got to ride (her, they).

6. (Us, We) had a lot of fun!

7. (They, It) was a great day on the farm.

Spectrum Language Arts
Grade 1
18
Review: Chapter 1 Lessons 3–5
Grammar: Parts of Speech

Review

Write an adjective to describe each noun. Remember to ask **What kind?** about each noun. The words in the box can give you some ideas. You can also use your own words.

Answers will vary. Possible answers:

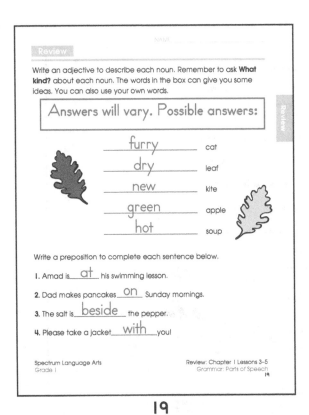

furry _____ cat
dry _____ leaf
new _____ kite
green _____ apple
hot _____ soup

Write a preposition to complete each sentence below.

1. Amad is ___at___ his swimming lesson.

2. Dad makes pancakes ___on___ Sunday mornings.

3. The salt is ___beside___ the pepper.

4. Please take a jacket ___with___ you!

Spectrum Language Arts
Grade 1
Review: Chapter 1 Lessons 3–5
Grammar: Parts of Speech
19

Lesson 1.6 Sentences

A **sentence** is a complete thought. It starts with a capital letter. It ends with an end mark.

(T)im plays ball(.)   (T)hat book is funny(.)   (L)ook at the frog(.)

Identify It
Look at each group of words. If it is a sentence, make a check mark ✔ on the line. Circle the capital letter. Circle the end mark.

1. ___✔___ (T)he fire truck is bright red(.)

2. _____ shiny and clean

3. _____ shows us the hoses

4. ___✔___ (I) can see the ladders on top(.)

5. ___✔___ (T)he siren is very loud(.)

6. _____ cover my ears

7. ___✔___ (W)e climb inside(.)

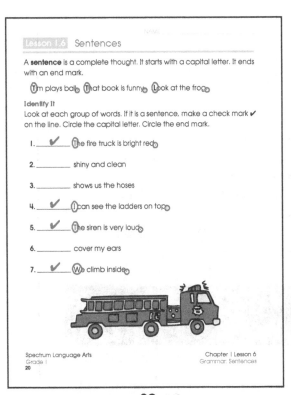

Spectrum Language Arts
Grade 1
20
Chapter 1 Lesson 6
Grammar: Sentences

Spectrum Language Arts
Grade 1

Lesson 1.6 Sentences

Rewrite It
Read each set of words below. Rewrite it as a sentence. Make sure to start with a capital and end with a period.

1. our fire station has a dog

   Our fire station has a dog.

2. he is white with black spots

   He is white with black spots.

3. his name is Charlie

   His name is Charlie.

4. he likes to ride in the truck

   He likes to ride in the truck.

Try It
Write two sentences about Charlie.

Answers will vary.

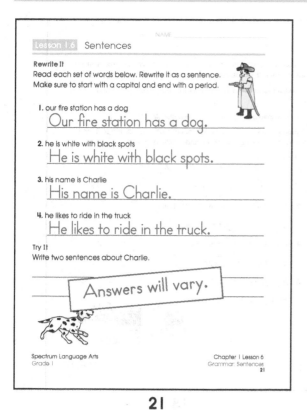

Spectrum Language Arts
Grade 1

Chapter 1 Lesson 6
Grammar: Sentences
21

21

Lesson 1.7 Statements

A **statement** is a telling sentence. It starts with a capital letter. It ends with a period.

(A)nton is in first grade(.) (D)inner is ready(.)

Proof It
Read each statement below. If it does not start with a capital, make three lines under the letter (≡). Write the capital letter above. If the period is missing, add it and circle it.

E
≡ella lost her pencil(.)

1. L
   ≡look outside on a clear, dark night.

2. You will see many stars(.)

3. T
   ≡they are very far away(.)

4. S
   ≡stars do not live forever.

5. Some groups of stars have names(.)

6. O
   ≡our sun is a star(.)

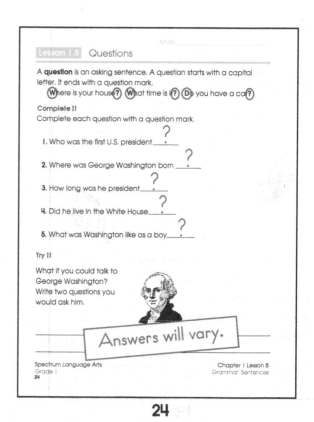

Spectrum Language Arts
Grade 1
22

Chapter 1 Lesson 7
Grammar: Sentences

22

Lesson 1.7 Statements

Rewrite It
Rewrite the sentences. Each should begin with a capital and end with a period.

1. jaya has a telescope

   Jaya has a telescope.

2. jaya likes to see the stars

   Jaya likes to see the stars.

3. she can find the Big Dipper

   She can find the Big Dipper.

4. dad showed her Venus

   Dad showed her Venus.

5. the moon is easy to spot

   The moon is easy to spot.

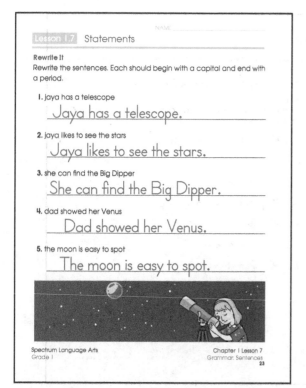

Spectrum Language Arts
Grade 1

Chapter 1 Lesson 7
Grammar: Sentences
23

23

Lesson 1.8 Questions

A **question** is an asking sentence. A question starts with a capital letter. It ends with a question mark.

(W)here is your house(?) (W)hat time is i(?) (D)o you have a ca(?)

Complete It
Complete each question with a question mark.

1. Who was the first U.S. president__?__

2. Where was George Washington born__?__

3. How long was he president__?__

4. Did he live in the White House__?__

5. What was Washington like as a boy__?__

Try It

What if you could talk to George Washington? Write two questions you would ask him.

Answers will vary.

Spectrum Language Arts
Grade 1
24

Chapter 1 Lesson 8
Grammar: Sentences

24

Lesson 1.8 Questions

Match It

Read each statement about the White House. Read the questions in the box. Write the letter of the question that matches each statement.

> **A.** How many rooms does it have?
>
> **B.** Who was first to live in it?
>
> **C.** How many chefs work there?
>
> **D.** Who named the White House?

1. __D__ Theodore Roosevelt named the White House.

2. __A__ It has 132 rooms.

3. __C__ Five chefs work at the White House.

4. __B__ John Adams was first to live in it.

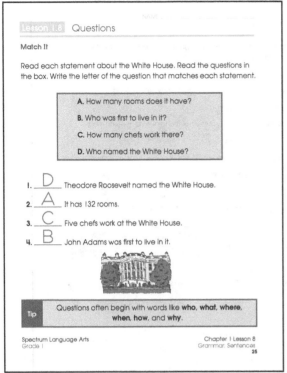

Tip	Questions often begin with words like **who, what, where, when, how,** and **why.**

Spectrum Language Arts
Grade 1

Chapter 1 Lesson 8
Grammar: Sentences
25

25

Lesson 1.9 Exclamations

An **exclamation** is a sentence that shows excitement. It can also show surprise. It starts with a capital letter. It ends with an exclamation point.

(I) need help(!) (We) won the game(!) (V)acation starts toda(y!)

Identify It
Read each pair of sentences. One sentence in each pair is a statement. The other sentence is an exclamation. Add the correct end marks.

1. I won the race __!__

   Today is Monday __.__

2. Finn is my best friend __.__

   Finn found ten dollars __!__

3. I have two sisters __.__

   Something is out there __!__

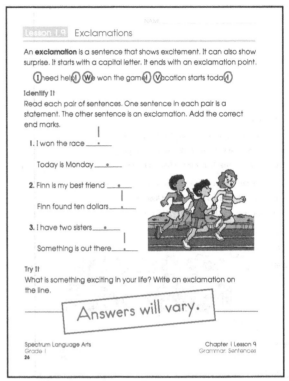

Try It
What is something exciting in your life? Write an exclamation on the line.

Answers will vary.

Spectrum Language Arts
Grade 1
26

Chapter 1 Lesson 9
Grammar: Sentences

26

Lesson 1.9 Exclamations

Rewrite It
Rewrite each exclamation on the line. Remember, start with a capital. End with an exclamation point.

1. the dog got out

   The dog got out!

2. don't knock over your cup

   Don't knock over your cup!

3. lena's painting came in first place

   Lena's painting came in first place!

4. i lost my first tooth

   I lost my first tooth!

Tip	Some exclamations are just one word. **Help! Wow! Great! Ouch!**

Spectrum Language Arts
Grade 1

Chapter 1 Lesson 9
Grammar: Sentences
27

27

Lesson 1.10 Combining Sentences

Sometimes, two sentences can be made into one. Both sentences must tell about the same thing.

> Frogs live in the pond. Fish live in the pond.

Use the word **and** to join the parts of the sentence.

> Frogs **and** fish live in the pond.

Complete It
Read the sentences.
Fill in the missing words.

1. Max went to the fair. Li went to the fair.

   Max ___and___ Li went to the fair.

2. Mom rode the Ferris wheel. Dad rode the Ferris wheel.

   ___Mom___ and Dad rode the Ferris wheel.

3. The juice was cold. The ice cream was cold.

   The juice and ___ice cream___ were cold.

4. Li played two games. Mom played two games.

   ___Li and___ and Mom played two games.

Spectrum Language Arts
Grade 1
28

Chapter 1 Lesson 10
Grammar: Sentences

28

Spectrum Language Arts
Grade 1

Lesson 1.10 Combining Sentences

Identify It
Read the letter. Three pairs of sentences can be joined. Underline each pair.

June 12, 2014

Dear Ana,

Guess what? We went to the fair. <u>I had fun. Marco had fun.</u> We went on lots of rides. <u>Tess stayed home. Jane stayed home.</u> They are too little for the fair.

<u>My ticket was lost. My money was lost.</u> Don't worry, I was lucky. Marco found them. I left them in a bumper car. It was a great day. I love the fair.

Hope to see you soon!

Your friend,

Will

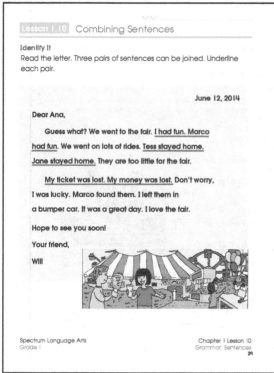

Spectrum Language Arts
Grade 1

Chapter 1 Lesson 10
Grammar: Sentences
29

29

Review

A **sentence** is a complete thought. It starts with a capital. It ends with an end mark.

(I)t is 4:00(.)

A **statement** is a telling sentence. It ends with a period.

(M)ia loves cheese(.)

A **question** is an asking sentence. It ends with a question mark.

(W)here are your shoes(?)

An **exclamation** shows excitement. It ends with an exclamation point.

(I) got stung by a bee(!)

Putting It Together

1. Look at the picture. Write a statement about it.

_____

2. Look at the pict~~ure~~

3. Look at the picture. Write an exclamation about it.

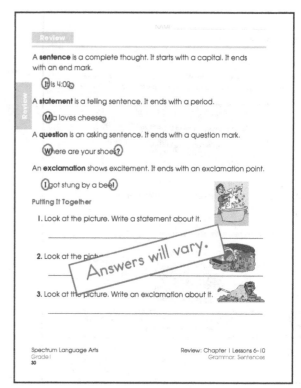

Answers will vary.

Spectrum Language Arts
Grade 1
30

Review: Chapter 1 Lessons 6–10
Grammar: Sentences

30

Review

Sometimes, two sentences can be joined. Use the word **and** to make two sentences into one.

Sara skates every week.   Kyle skates every week.

Sara **and** Kyle skate every week.

Rewrite each pair of sentences as one sentence.

1. Bears eat berries. Birds eat berries.
   Bears and birds eat berries.

2. Frogs like bugs. Toads like bugs.
   Frogs and toads like bugs.

3. Cows graze on hay. Horses graze on hay.
   Cows and horses graze on hay.

4. Mice eat acorns. Squirrels eat acorns.
   Mice and squirrels eat acorns.

Spectrum Language Arts
Grade 1

Review: Chapter 1 Lessons 6–10
Grammar: Sentences
31

31

Chapter 2 Mechanics
Lesson 2.1 Capitalizing the First Word in a Sentence

A sentence always begins with a capital letter. This shows that a new sentence is starting.

(W)hat is your name? (T)asha has two birds. (I) see the train!

Proof It
Look for the words that should be capitalized. Mark the letter with three lines below it (≡). Then, write the capital above it.

Example: $\underset{\equiv}{s}$onya will wear her red dress.

$\underset{\equiv}{b}$ats are odd animals. They fly like birds. $\underset{\equiv}{e}$ven so, they are not birds. Bats are mammals, like dogs and cats. $\underset{\equiv}{m}$ost bats eat bugs. $\underset{\equiv}{s}$ome eat fruit.

Bats sleep during the day. $\underset{\equiv}{t}$hey are awake at night. They do not see well. They make a very high sound. $\underset{\equiv}{t}$he sound bounces off things. This tells bats where things are. $\underset{\equiv}{i}$t helps them get around.

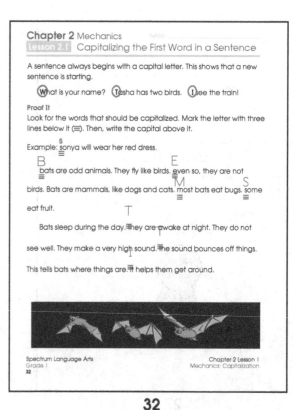

Spectrum Language Arts
Grade 1
32

Chapter 2 Lesson 1
Mechanics: Capitalization

32

Spectrum Language Arts
Grade 1

Answer Key

Lesson 2.1 Capitalizing the First Word in a Sentence

Rewrite It

Rewrite each sentence. Make sure to begin with a capital letter.

1. last week, a bat got in our house.

   Last week, a bat got in our house.

2. i didn't know what it was at first.

   I didn't know what it was at first.

3. mom caught it and let it go outside.

   Mom caught it and let it go outside.

4. that poor bat was scared!

   That poor bat was scared!

5. i don't think he'll be back.

   I don't think he'll be back.

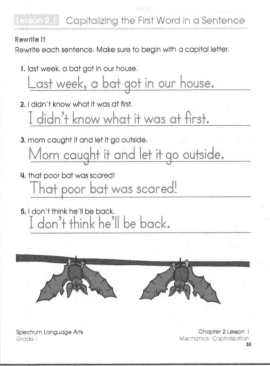

Spectrum Language Arts
Grade 1

Chapter 2 Lesson 1
Mechanics: Capitalization
33

33

Lesson 2.2 Capitalizing the Pronoun I

The pronoun I is always capitalized. It can start a sentence. It can be in the middle of a sentence.

   (I) like pears.   (I) will wear a jacket.   Min and (I) want to swing.

Proof It

Read the story. Each time you see the word I, make sure it is capitalized. If it is not, make three lines below it (≡). Then, write the capital above it.

Example: Lulu and i̲ went on a walk.

   Last week, i̲ went to the dentist. I was not nervous. i̲ was just getting a check-up. My sister had a tooth pulled once. Grace and i̲ were playing outside. She tripped and hit her mouth. I knew she needed help, so i̲ called for Mom. Mom and i̲ took Grace right to Dr. Cruz. i̲ told him what happened. Then, Mom and I sat with Grace. She was so brave! Her lip was puffy, but she was okay. Grace and i̲ will be more careful from now on!

Spectrum Language Arts
Grade 1
34

Chapter 2 Lesson 2
Mechanics: Capitalization

34

Lesson 2.2 Capitalizing the Pronoun I

Try It

Read each sentence below. Write the word I in the box. Fill in the other blank with a word that finishes the sentence.

1. [I] like to eat Answers will vary .

2. Answers will vary and play catch.

3. [I] like the color Answers will vary .

4. Each weekend, [I] go Answers will vary .

5. My Answers will vary and [I] like to read books together.

6. [I] have a cool Answers will vary .

Spectrum Language Arts
Grade 1

Chapter 2 Lesson 2
Mechanics: Capitalization
35

35

Review

A sentence always begins with a capital letter.

   (I)s that your train?   (L)et's plant the flowers.

The pronoun I is always spelled with a capital letter.

   (I) forgot my lunch!   (L)ucy and I baked bread.

Look for the words that should be capitalized. Mark the letter with three lines below it (≡). Then, write the capital above it.

1. M̲y best friend, Harry, has a fish tank.

2. H̲arry and i̲ went to the pet store.

3. H̲e wanted to buy some fish food.

4. I̲ like to look at all kinds of fish.

5. M̲om says my sister and i̲ can get a small tank next year.

6. O̲range clownfish are the ones i̲ like best.

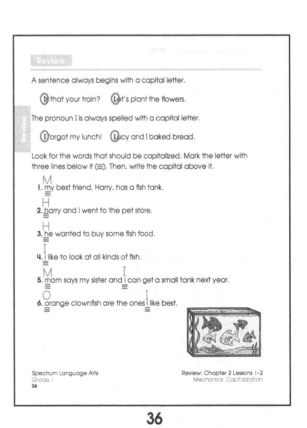

Spectrum Language Arts
Grade 1
36

Review: Chapter 2 Lessons 1–2
Mechanics: Capitalization

36

Spectrum Language Arts
Grade 1

Page 37

Review

Rewrite each sentence. Make sure to use capitals where they are needed.

1. i have a new, red bike.

   I have a new, red bike.

2. my bike has a bell and a basket.

   My bike has a bell and a basket.

3. ali and i ride to the library.

   Ali and I ride to the library.

Read each question. Answer it with a sentence that starts with I.

1. How old are you?

2. What is your favorite food?

3. What is one ____ like to do in the summer?

Answers will vary.

37

Page 38

Lesson 2.3 Capitalizing Names

Names begin with a capital letter. A person's name starts with a capital letter. A pet's name starts with a capital letter, too.

My sister's name is (E)mma.   I have a cat named (S)ocks.

Match It
The child and pet in each picture need a name. Choose a set of names from the box. Write them next to the picture. Make sure you start each name with a capital letter.

| lily and lucky | carlos and coco | |
| ben and bubbles | greg and gus | stella and star |

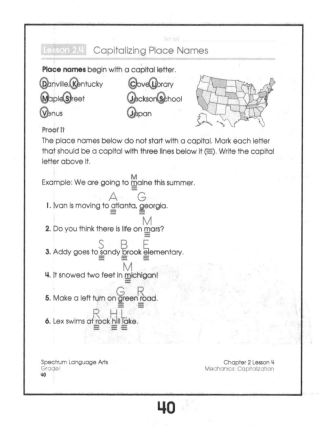

_____ and _____

_____ and _____

Order of answers will vary.

_____ and _____

38

Page 39

Lesson 2.3 Capitalizing Names

Proof It
The names below do not start with a capital letter. Find each letter that should be a capital letter. Make three lines below it (≡). Then, write the capital letter above it.

1. luke, jay, and Leo are all sam's brothers.
   L   J   S

2. Lu named the kittens bella and sassy.
                       B   S

3. saw his friend ava at the park.
                   A

4. jess got to milk millie and Bonnie at the farm.
   J   M

Try It
Write a sentence about two of your ____ ____ es in the senten ____

Answers will vary.

39

Page 40

Lesson 2.4 Capitalizing Place Names

Place names begin with a capital letter.

(D)anville, (K)entucky   (C)ove (L)ibrary
(M)aple (S)treet   (J)ackson (S)chool
(V)enus   (J)apan

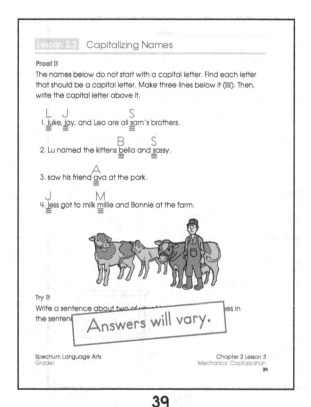

Proof It
The place names below do not start with a capital. Mark each letter that should be a capital with three lines below it (≡). Write the capital letter above it.

Example: We are going to maine this summer.
                              M

1. Ivan is moving to atlanta, georgia.
                     A   G

2. Do you think there is life on mars?
                                 M

3. Addy goes to sandy brook elementary.
                 S   B   E

4. It snowed two feet in michigan!
                         M

5. Make a left turn on green road.
                       G   R

6. Lex swims at rock hill lake.
                R   H L

40

Lesson 2.4 Capitalizing Place Names

Try It

Answer each question. Make sure to start each place name with a capital letter.

1. What is the name of your street?

_____

2. What city were you born in?

_____

3. What is a state you wou~~~

4. What coun~~~ ou live in?

_____

5. What is the name of a place you go a lot? It could be a school. Maybe it is a store or a library.

_____

Answers will vary.

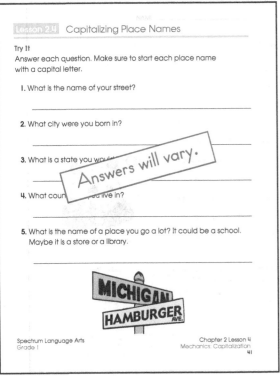

41

Lesson 2.5 Capitalizing Days and Months

The **days of the week** start with a capital letter.

(M)onday, (T)uesday, (W)ednesday, (T)hursday, (F)riday, (S)aturday, Sunday

The **months of the year** start with a capital letter, too.

(J)anuary, February, (M)arch, (A)pril, (M)ay, (J)une, July, (A)ugust, (S)eptember, (O)ctober, (N)ovember, (D)ecember

Solve It

Read each clue. Write the day of the week that matches it. Use the list above.

1. People like me a lot. I am the first day of the weekend.
   Saturday

2. I am the first weekday. My name starts with **m**. Monday

3. You can find the word **sun** hiding in my name. Sunday

4. I am the last weekday. Here comes the weekend!
   Friday

5. I come in the middle of the week. My name starts with **w**.
   Wednesday

6. My name starts with **t**. I come near the end of the week.
   Thursday

7. My name starts with **t**, too. I come near the start of the week.
   Tuesday

42

Lesson 2.5 Capitalizing Days and Months

Complete It

Fill in the month in each sentence. Make sure to use a capital letter.

1. (june)   Julia's birthday is in   June

2. (april)   Andy ate apples in   April

3. (july)   Jake plays jacks in   July

4. (may)   Mira met Matt in   May

5. (october)   Olly saw an owl in   October

6. (september) Sam swam in   September

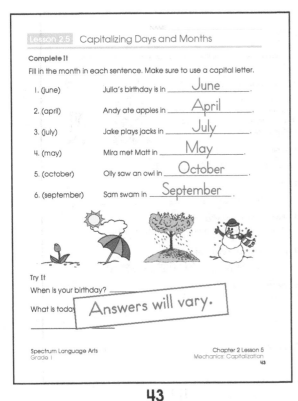

Try It

When is your birthday?

What is today ~~~

Answers will vary.

_____

43

Review

Names of people and pets start with a capital letter.

Give the book to (M)alik. Let's name the fish (B)uddy and (G)izmo.

Names of special places start with a capital letter, too.

(D)anville (H)ospital   (C)ap's (T)oy (S)tore

(C)hicago   (M)exico

Putting It Together

Complete each sentence with the word in the box. Make sure you begin names with a capital letter.

1. lita   Rico and   Lita   were on vacation.

2. cape cod   Their family was going to   Cape Cod

3. sofia and joe   Cousins   Sofia and Joe   were coming, too.

4. tucker   Tucker   , the poodle, rode on Mom's lap.

5. dixie   The family cat,   Dixie   , stayed home.

6. clean spoon diner   Dad stopped to get lunch at the   Clean Spoon Diner

44

Review

Days of the week start with a capital letter.

(T)uesday (S)aturday (W)ednesday

Months of the year start with a capital letter, too.

(M)arch (J)une (O)ctober

The days and months below do not start with a capital. Mark each letter that should be a capital with three lines below it (≡). Write the capital letter above it.

1. M͟onday, M͟arch 8 is Eli's birthday.

2. Clare's dance is on S͟aturday night.

3. It snowed on T͟uesday and W͟ednesday.

4. My mom and dad were both born on D͟ecember 2.

5. Kenji will be 7 on F͟riday, A͟pril 20.

6. The store will open in S͟eptember.

7. I saw a full moon on M͟onday, J͟uly 11.

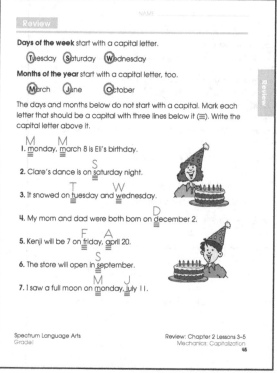

Spectrum Language Arts
Grade1

Review: Chapter 2 Lessons 3-5
Mechanics: Capitalization
45

45

A **period** is an end mark. It comes at the end of a sentence.

I have a hole in my pants(.) Luis has a loose tooth(.)

Complete It
Each sentence below is missing a period. Add it and circle it.

Example: Turn on the lights(.)

1. Giant pandas are found in China(.)

2. They live in the mountains(.)

3. There are not many pandas left in the wild(.)

4. Pandas have black rings around their eyes(.)

5. They can weigh 250 pounds(.)

6. Pandas eat bamboo(.)

7. They get most of their water from bamboo(.)

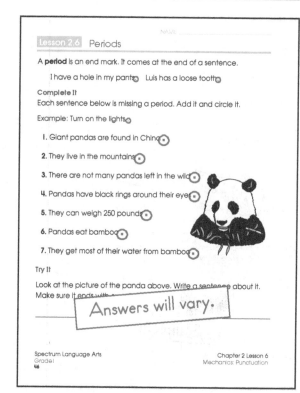

Try It

Look at the picture of the panda above. Write a sentence about it. Make sure it ends with

Answers will vary.

Spectrum Language Arts
Grade1
46

Chapter 2 Lesson 6
Mechanics: Punctuation

46

Lesson 2.6 Periods

Tip A capital letter can show you where a new sentence start.

Proof It
The periods are missing in the paragraph. Add them and circle them.

Baby pandas are called cubs(.) A new baby is very small(.) It is about the size of a stick of butter(.) The cubs are not black and white(.) They are pink(.) A new cub looks more like a mouse than a bear(.) It has almost no hair(.)

A baby panda can not do much at first(.) The baby's eyes stay shut for 6 to 8 weeks(.) It takes a few months for a cub to learn to walk(.) Baby pandas need their moms, just like baby humans(.)

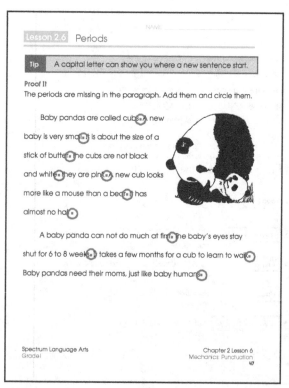

Spectrum Language Arts
Grade1

Chapter 2 Lesson 6
Mechanics: Punctuation
47

47

Lesson 2.7 Question Marks

A **question mark** comes at the end of a question. It shows where the question ends.

Can you play checkers(?) Where is my red bow(?) Have you seen Erin(?)

Rewrite It
Rewrite each question. Make sure it starts with a capital letter and ends with a question mark.

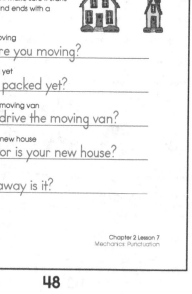

1. where are you moving
Where are you moving?

2. have you packed yet
Have you packed yet?

3. who will drive the moving van
Who will drive the moving van?

4. what color is your new house
What color is your new house?

5. how far away is it
How far away is it?

Spectrum Language Arts
Grade 1
48

Chapter 2 Lesson 7
Mechanics: Punctuation

48

Lesson 2.7 Question Marks

Identify It

Read each pair of sentences. Add a period after each statement. Add a question mark after each question. Underline the word that tells you the sentence is a question.

1. <u>What</u> is your new address?

   It is 811 Elm Street.

2. I can't find my roller skates.

   Have you seen them?

3. <u>What</u> school do you go to?

   I go to Shady Lane School.

4. Nick and Izzy live next door.

   <u>Who</u> lives in the blue house?

5. <u>Why</u> are you moving?

   My mom got a new job.

49

Lesson 2.8 Exclamation Points

An **exclamation point** comes at the end of an exclamation. An exclamation is a sentence that shows excitement. It can also show surprise.

That's great news!   Look at the snake!   We won!

Identify It

Read each pair of sentences. Add a period after each statement. Add an exclamation point after each exclamation.

1. Today is Saturday.

   It rained four inches today!

2. Don't forget your umbrella!

   Jon has a green umbrella.

3. Watch out for that branch!

   Dad will pick up the branches.

4. Jaya did not step in the puddle.

   My book fell in the puddle!

50

Lesson 2.8 Exclamation Points

Try It

Look at each picture. Write an exclamation to go with it. Begin with a capital letter. End with an exclamation point.

Answers will vary.

51

Review

A statement ends with a **period**.

   Aunt Kimm made pasta for dinner.

A question ends with a **question mark**.

   How far away is Mars?

An exclamation ends with an **exclamation point**.

   I smell smoke!

Putting It Together

Answers will vary. Possible answers:

Example: Question: What day is it?   Today is Monday.

1. Question: What is her name?

   Her name is Jazmin.

2. Question: Where is the book?

   The book is on the desk.

3. Question: How old are you?

   I am six.

4. Question: What color is the ball?

   The ball is green.

52

Page 53

Review

Read the letter. It is missing some end marks. Add three periods, three question marks, and two exclamation points.

Dear Owen,

How are you doing**?** I am fine. Mom, Kate, and I went on a picnic yesterday. Have you ever been to Falls River Park**?** It is beautiful**.**

We brought a blanket to sit on**.** I spread it out. Kate got the basket. Then, she sat down on the blanket. Guess what happened**?** She got stung by a bee! Mom got the stinger out**.** Kate did not even cry.

We ate our bread and cheese. We had some fruit and cookies, too**.** After we ate, we played catch. What a fun picnic**!**

Your friend,

Noah

Spectrum Language Arts
Grade 1

Chapter 2 Lessons 6-8
Mechanics: Capitalization
53

Page 54

Lesson 2.9 Commas with Dates

A **comma** is a punctuation mark. In a date, it goes between the day and the year.

June 20**,** 1973   October 6**,** 2006   April 4**,** 1866

If a comma is missing, use this mark (∧) to add it.

March 17∧2014

Proof It

Commas are missing from the dates below. Use this mark (∧) to add them.

1. John moved to New York on December 23∧1982.

2. Aunt Keiko was born on February 19∧1979.

3. Grandma and Grandpa got married on May 6∧1960.

4. I met Jada on July 11∧2008.

5. Riley's birthday is August 14∧2004.

Try It

When were you born? Write the date on the line._____

Ask a friend when he or she was born. Write the date on the line.

_____

Spectrum Language Arts
Grade 1
54

Chapter 2 Lesson 9
Mechanics: Punctuation

Page 55

Lesson 2.9 Commas with Dates

Rewrite It

Rewrite each date. Use commas where they are needed.

1. January 5 1984   January 5, 1984
2. November 18 2002   November 18, 2002
3. May 23 1999   May 23, 1999
4. February 9 2015   February 9, 2015
5. July 31 1944   July 31, 1944
6. September 12 1965   September 12, 1965
7. April 29 1814   April 29, 1814

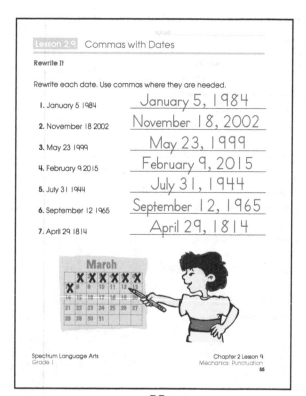

Spectrum Language Arts
Grade 1

Chapter 2 Lesson 9
Mechanics: Punctuation
55

Page 56

Lesson 2.10 Commas with Cities and States

A **comma** is used between the name of a city and state.

Detroit**,** Michigan   Wilmington**,** Delaware   Portland**,** Oregon

Proof It
Add a comma between each city and state. Use this mark (∧) to add each comma.

1. You may have heard of Chicago∧Illinois.

2. You might know Dallas∧Texas.

3. Have you heard of Chicken∧Alaska?

4. Would you like to go to Bumble Bee∧Arizona?

5. How about Two Egg∧Florida?

6. Is it boring to live in Boring∧Maryland?

7. What is it like in Moon∧Virginia?

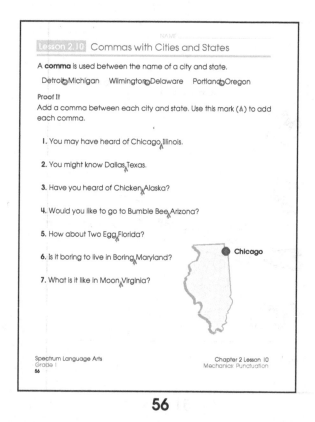

Chicago

Spectrum Language Arts
Grade 1
56

Chapter 2 Lesson 10
Mechanics: Punctuation

Lesson 2.10 Commas with Cities and States

Complete It
Finish each sentence with a city and state from the box. Use commas where they are needed.

Order of answers will vary.

1. Anton is moving to Lima, Ohio.

2. In May, Izzy will go to Macon, Georgia.

3. Lee's aunt lives in Reno, Nevada.

4. It will take Cam two days to drive to Portland, Maine.

5. Dan found Austin, Texas on the map.

6. Jane has lived in Miami, Florida for 11 years.

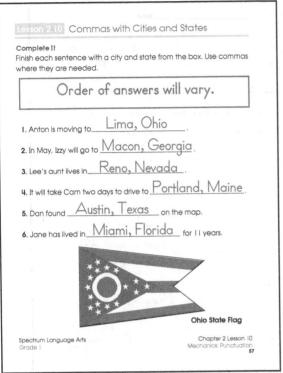

Ohio State Flag

Spectrum Language Arts
Grade 1

Chapter 2 Lesson 10
Mechanics: Punctuation
57

57

Lesson 2.11 Apostrophes with Possessives

An **apostrophe plus s ('s)** shows that someone owns something.

Keisha's book   Meg's brush   Cody's train

Complete It
Add **'s** to each blank below. Make a line under the item each person owns.

1. Emma __'s__ <u>drawing</u>

2. Diego __'s__ <u>pen</u>

3. Mr. Stein __'s__ <u>truck</u>

4. Dante __'s__ <u>leaf</u>

5. Kat __'s__ <u>frog</u>

6. Jen __'s__ <u>apple</u>

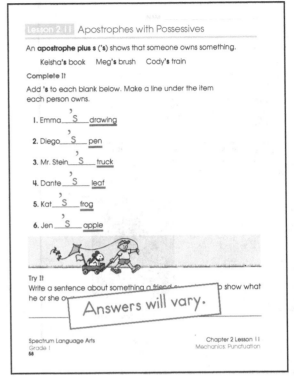

Try It
Write a sentence about something a friend o___ ___ to show what he or she o___

Answers will vary.

Spectrum Language Arts
Grade 1

Chapter 2 Lesson 11
Mechanics: Punctuation
58

58

Lesson 2.11 Apostrophes with Possessives

Identify It
Read each pair of sentences. Make a check mark ✔ next to the one that is correct.

1. ✔ Mia's hat

___ Mias hat

2. ___ Blakes bird'

✔ Blake's bird

3. ✔ Amad's boots

___ Amads boots

4. ___ Rosas muffin

✔ Rosa's muffin

5. ___ Nicks snake'

✔ Nick's snake

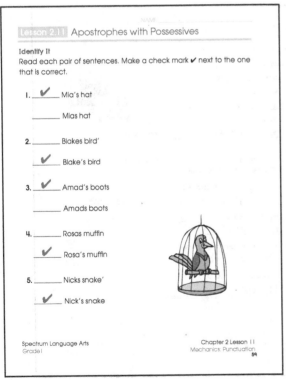

Spectrum Language Arts
Grade 1

Chapter 2 Lesson 11
Mechanics: Punctuation
59

59

Review

In a date, use a comma between the day and the month.

April 5, 1988   December 20, 2015   June 13, 2001

Use a comma between the name of a city and state.

St. Paul, Minnesota   Buffalo, New York   Nashville, Tennessee

Use this mark (∧) to add the missing commas.

1. My grandma was born on January 24, 1936.

2. Chris sent a letter to Wichita, Kansas.

3. How old will you be on January 1, 2020?

4. A big snow storm hit Augusta, Maine.

5. We stayed at a hotel in Madison, Wisconsin.

6. The baby turned one on August 23, 2009.

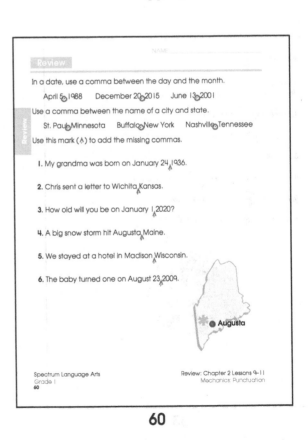

● Augusta

Spectrum Language Arts
Grade 1

Review: Chapter 2 Lessons 9–11
Mechanics: Punctuation
60

60

Page 61

Review

An **apostrophe plus s** ('s) shows that someone owns something.

Manny's house   Lily's duck   Carter's pail

Pick one word from Box 1 and one from Box 2. Write a possessive using your words.

| Box 1 | Tony | Zack | Dan |
| | Ella | Ming | Maria |

| Box 2 | sock | sled | drum |
| | map | fish | doll |

Answers will vary. Possible answers:

1. Tony's sock
2. Ella's map
3. Zack's sled
4. Ming's fish
5. Dan's drum
6. Maria's doll

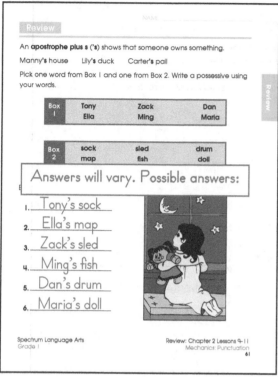

Spectrum Language Arts
Grade 1

Review: Chapter 2 Lessons 9–11
Mechanics: Punctuation
61

61

Page 62

Chapter 3 Usage
Lesson 3.1 Subject-Verb Agreement

When a sentence is about one person or thing, add **s** to the verb.

Jim drops the ball.   The leaf blows away.

When a sentence is about more than one person or thing, do not add **s**.

The cats look for mice.   Jeff and Yoko play the piano.

Match It
Draw a line to match each sentence to the correct ending.

1. Ms. Ito — grades the tests.
   grade the tests.

2. The pencils — fall on the floor.
   falls on the floor.

3. The bell — ring at 3:00.
   rings at 3:00.

4. The girls — paints in the art room.
   paint in the art room.

5. Caleb — sings after school.
   sing after school.

Spectrum Language Arts
Grade 1

Chapter 3 Lesson 1
Usage
62

62

Page 63

Lesson 3.1 Subject-Verb Agreement

Complete It
Circle the word that completes each sentence.

1. Max (puts, put) on his space suit.
2. He (slip, slips) on the boots.
3. The helmet (roll, rolls) across the floor.
4. Max and his dog (travel, travels) to outer space.
5. They (sees, see) Earth from far above.
6. Max's mom (calls, call) him home for dinner.

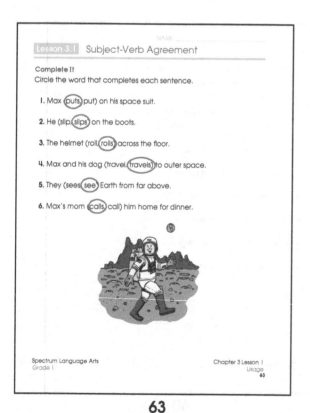

Spectrum Language Arts
Grade 1

Chapter 3 Lesson 1
Usage
63

63

Page 64

Lesson 3.2 Irregular Verbs: **Am, Is, Are**

The words **am**, **is**, and **are** are all verbs.
Use **am** with the word **I**.

I **am** happy.   I **am** cold.
Use **is** with one person or thing.

The balloon **is** red.   Seth **is** at the park.
Use **are** with more than one person or thing.

The pens **are** in my desk.   The boys **are** inside.

Rewrite It
Each sentence below has the wrong verb. Rewrite it with the correct verb. Choose from **is**, **am**, or **are**.

1. The farmer am ready to milk the cows.
   The farmer is ready to milk the cows.
2. I is glad to help Bill.
   I am glad to help Bill.
3. The horse are brown and white.
   The horse is brown and white.
4. The kids is by the pond.
   The kids are by the pond.

Spectrum Language Arts
Grade 1

Chapter 3 Lesson 2
Usage
64

64

Lesson 3.2 Irregular Verbs: **Am, Is, Are**

Complete It
Complete each sentence with the correct word from the box. Write it on the line.

1. is are   The pig _____ is _____ in the mud.

2. am are   I _____ am _____ sure I let the dog out.

3. is are   The ducks _____ are _____ with their babies.

4. am is   The cow _____ is _____ next to the fence.

5. are is   Farmer Bill and Henry _____ are _____ in the kitchen.

6. is are   The pony _____ is _____ six months old.

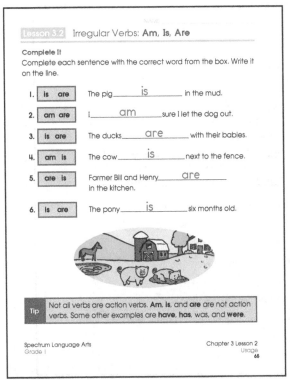

| Tip | Not all verbs are action verbs. **Am, is,** and **are** are not action verbs. Some other examples are **have, has,** was, and **were.** |

65

Lesson 3.3 Past-Tense Verbs: **Was, Were**

The words **was** and **were** tell about something that happened in the past.

Use **was** with one person or thing.

The bike **was** broken.   I **was** ready for dinner.

Use **were** with more than one person or thing.

Amit and Liza **were** at the movies.   The books **were** in the car.

Proof It
Read each sentence. Check to see if the verbs **was** and **were** are correct. If you find a mistake, cross it out. Write the correct word above it.

Example: The worm ~~were~~ **was** under the leaf.

1. The parade ~~were~~ **was** at 1:00.

2. The kids ~~was~~ **were** excited to see it.

3. The balloons were red, yellow, and green.

4. The band ~~were~~ **was** very loud.

5. Drew and Maggy ~~was~~ **were** in the first float.

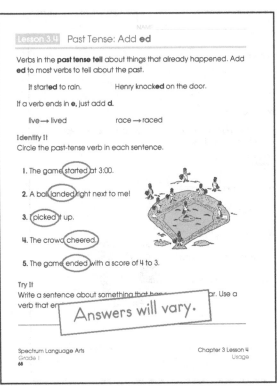

66

Lesson 3.3 Past-Tense Verbs: **Was, Were**

Complete It
Fill in each blank with **was** or **were**.

1. The drums _____ were _____ in the middle of the parade.

2. It _____ was _____ a sunny day.

3. We _____ were _____ lucky it didn't rain.

4. Mom and Dad _____ were _____ on the sidewalk.

5. Nico _____ was _____ the leader.

6. At the end of the parade, we _____ were _____ tired!

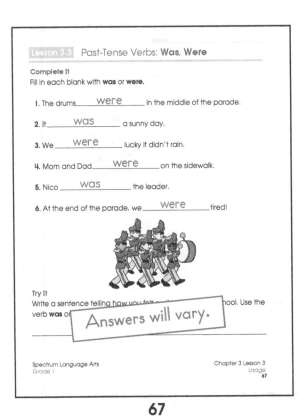

Try It
Write a sentence telling how you felt ~~at~~ ~~school.~~ Use the verb **was** or ~~~~   Answers will vary.

67

Lesson 3.4 Past Tense: Add **ed**

Verbs in the **past tense tell** about things that already happened. Add **ed** to most verbs to tell about the past.

It start**ed** to rain.   Henry knock**ed** on the door.

If a verb ends in **e**, just add **d**.

live → lived   race → raced

Identify It
Circle the past-tense verb in each sentence.

1. The game (started) at 3:00.

2. A ball (landed) right next to me!

3. I (picked) it up.

4. The crowd (cheered).

5. The game (ended) with a score of 4 to 3.

Try It
Write a sentence about something that ~~happened~~ ~~~~ ar. Use a verb that en~~~~   Answers will vary.

68

NAME _____

Lesson 3.4 Past Tense: Add **ed**

Complete It

Complete each sentence with the verb in the box. Add **d** or **ed** to put it in the past tense.

1. look — The pitcher ___looked___ at the batter.

2. wait — We ___waited___ to see the hit.

3. race — The player ___raced___ to first base.

4. jump — Number 3 ___jumped___ up to catch the ball.

5. sail — The ball ___sailed___ over the fence.

6. smile — I ___smiled___ at my brother.

7. want — We ___wanted___ to see a great game, and we did!

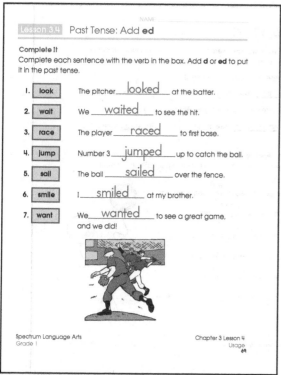

Spectrum Language Arts
Grade 1

Chapter 3 Lesson 4
Usage
69

69

NAME _____

Review

When a sentence is about one person or thing, add **s** to the verb.

Aunt Lola cut(**s**) my hair.

When a sentence is about more than one person or thing, do not add **s**.

The bears look for berries.

Use the verb **am** with the word I.   I **am** hiding.

Use the verbs **is** and **was** with one person or thing.

The pear **is** green.   Mr. Otis **was** sick today.

Use the verbs **are** or **were** with more than one person or thing.

The balls **are** in the gym.   The girls **were** smiling.

Putting It Together

Circle the word that completes each sentence.

1. The storm (is, are) getting closer.

2. I (am, is) not afraid of thunder.

3. The lights (blinks, blink) on and off.

4. Dad (light, lights) some candles.

5. My sisters and I (feel, feels) so cozy.

6. Once, we (was, were) without power for three days!

Spectrum Language Arts
Grade 1
70

Review: Chapter 3 Lessons 1-4
Usage

70

NAME _____

Review

Add **ed** to most verbs to tell about the past.

Ari kick**ed** the ball.

If a verb ends in **e**, just add **d**.

bake→baked

All the verbs in **bold** should be in the past tense. Cross them out. Write the correct verb above them.

1. It ~~snow~~ *snowed* all night.

2. Eva and I ~~look~~ *looked* out the window.

3. We ~~climb~~ *climbed* to the top of the hill.

4. We ~~skate~~ *skated* on the pond.

5. Mom ~~cook~~ *cooked* hot soup for lunch.

6. I ~~hope~~ *hoped* it would snow again!

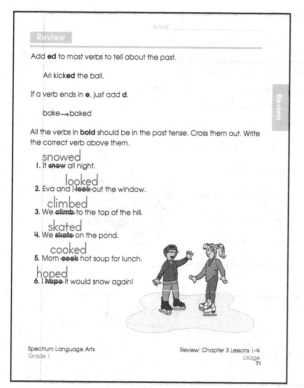

Spectrum Language Arts
Grade 1

Review: Chapter 3 Lessons 1-4
Usage
71

71

NAME _____

Lesson 3.5 Contractions with **Not**

A **contraction** is a way to join two words together. It is a shorter way to say something. An apostrophe (') takes the place of the missing letters.

Here are some contractions with **not**.

is not = isn't	are not = aren't
was not = wasn't	were not = weren't
does not = doesn't	did not = didn't
have not = haven't	can not = can't

Identify It

Read each sentence below. On the line, write a contraction for the underlined words.

1. I <u>can not</u> wait to go bowling. ___can't___

2. I <u>have not</u> ever gone before. ___haven't___

3. Mom said <u>it is not</u> easy to knock over all the pins. ___isn't___

4. It <u>was not</u> hard to pick a ball. ___wasn't___

5. There <u>were not</u> too many that fit my hand. ___weren't___

6. We <u>are not</u> going to be home by bedtime! ___aren't___

Spectrum Language Arts
Grade 1
72

Chapter 3 Lesson 5
Usage

72

Lesson 3.5 Contractions with **Not**

Match It
Draw a line to match each pair of words to its contraction.

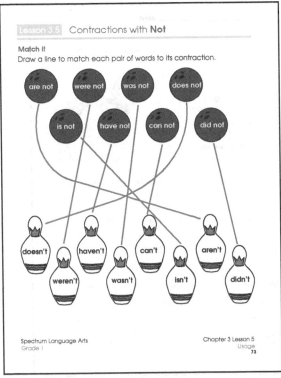

73

Lesson 3.6 Plurals with **s**

Plural means **more than one**. To make most nouns plural, just add **s**.

one hand → two hands   one plane → four planes
one tent → six tents   one hen → twelve hens

Solve It
Write the plural of each word on the line.
Then, circle the plurals in the puzzle.

bug _bugs_   spider _spiders_
beetle _beetles_ cricket _crickets_
wasp _wasps_   ant _ants_

e	q	c	b	u	g	s
z	a	r	f	b	j	l
s	p	i	d	e	r	s
w	m	c	q	e	x	p
d	m	k	p	t	k	p
i	y	e	v	l	g	g
a	n	t	s	e	e	d
w	a	s	p	s	n	u

74

Lesson 3.6 Plurals with **s**

Complete It
Add an **s** to each noun to make it plural.

1. Sanj found three ladybug _S_ .

2. Draw that moth with your marker _S_ .

3. Did you see the bee _S_ fly back to their hive?

4. Jose saw four slug _S_ in the garden.

5. Our dog _S_ get fleas every summer.

6. Watch out for tick _S_ in the woods!

7. Five inchworm _S_ crawled up the leaf.

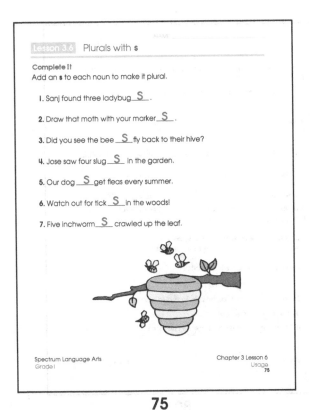

75

Lesson 3.7 Irregular Plural Nouns

For some words, do not add s to make the plural. Instead, the whole word changes.

One	More Than One
goose	geese
man	men
woman	women
tooth	teeth
child	children
mouse	mice
foot	feet

Other words do not change at all. Use the same word for one and more than one.

one deer→ five deer   one fish→ ten fish
one sheep→ three sheep   one moose→ eight moose

Look at each picture. Circle the word that names the picture.

deers	(deer)	feet	(foot)
(woman)	women	(children)	child
gooses	(geese)	(moose)	mooses

76

Lesson 3.7 Irregular Plural Nouns

Solve It
Look at each number and picture below. Fill in the missing word on the line. Choose from the words in the box.

mouse	men	fish
sheep	mice	teeth

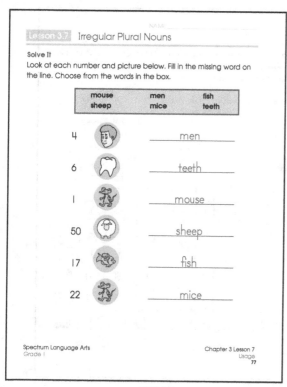

4   men

6   teeth

1   mouse

50   sheep

17   fish

22   mice

Spectrum Language Arts
Grade 1

Chapter 3 Lesson 7
Usage
77

77

Lesson 3.8 Prefixes and Suffixes

A **prefix** is added to the beginning of a root word. It changes the word's meaning.

The prefix **un** means **not** or **opposite of**.
Example: **un**healthy = **not** healthy

The prefix **re** means **again**.
Example: **re**wash = wash **again**

A **suffix** is added to the end of a root word. It changes the word's meaning.

The suffix **er** means **one who**.
Example: bak**er** = one who bakes

The suffix **ed** means that something happened **in the past**. (Remember, if a word ends in **e**, just add **d**).
Example: <u>Yesterday</u>, Luis wash**ed** the dog.

Match It
On the line, write a word with a suffix to match each meaning.

1. read again= reread

2. opposite of dress= undress

3. not sure= unsure

4. copy again= recopy

5. told again= retell

6. not able= unable

7. fill again= refill

Spectrum Language Arts
Grade 1

Chapter 3 Lesson 8
Usage
78

78

Lesson 3.8 Prefixes and Suffixes

Complete It
Each **bold** word is missing a suffix. Add the suffix **er** or **ed**. Use the meaning of the sentence to decide which one to add.

1. Riley wants to be a **paint** er one day.

2. Kris **smile** d at the baby.

3. Lena **tuck** ed her doll into bed.

4. The **catch** er stands behind home plate.

5. Mom handed a check to the **bank** er .

Sort the words in the box. Write them under the correct headings.

reuse	liked	unhurt	farmer
singer	resell	fixed	unfair

Words with Prefixes   Words with Suffixes
    reuse   liked
    unhurt   farmer
    resell   singer
    unfair   fixed

Spectrum Language Arts
Grade 1

Chapter 3 Lesson 8
Usage
79

79

Review

A **contraction** is a way to join two words together. An apostrophe (') takes the place of the missing letters.

is not = isn't   are not = aren't   was not = wasn't

Putting It Together
Read each pair of words. Write a sentence using a contraction for those words.

1. **is not** Answers will vary but should include isn't .

2. **did not** Answers will vary but should include didn't.

3. **was not** Answers will vary but should include wasn't

A **prefix** is added to the beginning of a root word. A **suffix** is added to the end of root word. Prefixes and suffixes change a word's meaning.

un = **not** or **opposite of**   **re** = **again**
er = **one who**   **ed** = **in the past**

Circle a prefix and a suffix in each item.

1. Did the bak(er)(re)heat the pizza?

2. Tia was(un)happy that the play last(ed)so long.

3. The build(er)sand(ed)all the wood.

4. Mac skat(ed)to the bench to(un)tie his laces.

Spectrum Language Arts
Grade 1

Review: Chapter 3 Lessons 5–8
Usage
80

80

Spectrum Language Arts
Grade 1

Page 81

Review

Plural means **more than one**. To make most nouns plural, just add **s**.

stamp → stamp(s)   cat → cat(s)

For some words, do not add **s** to make the plural. Instead, the whole word changes.

foot → feet   woman → women

Other words do not change at all. Use the same word for one and more than one.

one sheep → four sheep   one moose → six moose

Look at each word. Write the plural on the matching sock.

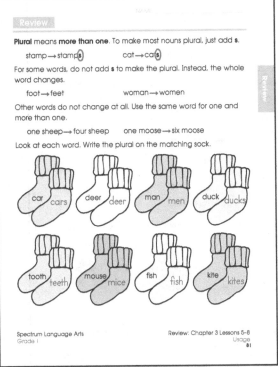

car / cars   deer / deer   man / men   duck / ducks

tooth / teeth   mouse / mice   fish / fish   kite / kites

Spectrum Language Arts
Grade 1

Review: Chapter 3 Lessons 5–8
Usage
81

81

Page 82

Lesson 3.9 Pronouns **I** and **Me**

You use the words **I** and **me** to talk about yourself.

I like bananas.   Amit gave **me** a new book.

When you talk about yourself and another person, put them first.

Devon and I ride the bus.   Eli made dinner for **Dad and me**.

Identify It
Circle **I** or **me** for each sentence.

1. (I, me) take piano lessons on Tuesdays.

2. Ms. Hawk gave (I, me) a gold star today.

3. (I, me) like to sing and play.

4. Mom asked (I, me) to play for Aunt Clare.

5. Aunt Clare told (I, me) that I play very well.

6. (I, me) want to play in a recital this spring.

Spectrum Language Arts
Grade 1
82

Chapter 3 Lesson 9
Usage

82

Page 83

Lesson 3.9 Pronouns **I** and **Me**

Complete It
Read the story. Write **I** or **me** in each blank to complete the sentences.

___I___ play the violin. My grandma gave ___me___ one. It was hers. ___I___ have a picture of her playing it. She told ___me___ to practice every day.

My friend Avi and ___I___ take lessons. I started when ___I___ was three. He and ___I___ like to play together. He told ___me___ he wants to play the piano, too. My grandma says she can teach Avi and ___me___.

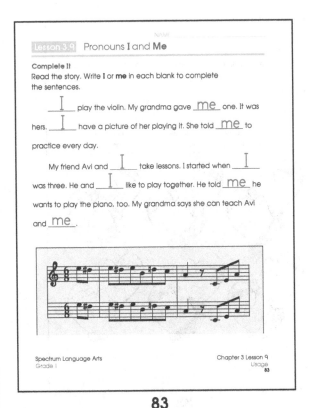

Spectrum Language Arts
Grade 1

Chapter 3 Lesson 9
Usage
83

83

Page 84

Lesson 3.10 Comparative Adjectives

Some adjectives are used to compare. Add **er** to an adjective to compare two things. Add **est** to compare three or more things.

Joe's dog is small.
Tasha's dog is small**er**.
Anton's dog is small**est**.

Identify It
Read the sentences. Choose the correct adjective from the box. Write it on the line.

1. oldest older | Sami is the ___oldest___ of all her sisters.

2. softer softest | Lola's pillow is ___softer___ than mine.

3. louder loudest | My alarm clock is ___louder___ than yours.

4. shorter shortest | Max has the ___shortest___ hair of all.

5. slow slowest | Kiku's turtle is ___slower___ than Alex's turtle.

Try It
Write two sentences. Compare two things in each sentence. Use these adjectives or one of your own: **harder, fastest, coldest, darker, youngest, longer**.

1. _____
2. _____

Answers will vary.

Spectrum Language Arts
Grade 1
84

Chapter 3 Lesson 10
Usage

84

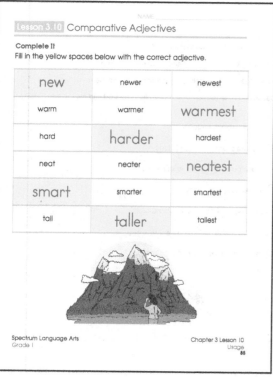

Lesson 3.10 Comparative Adjectives

Complete It
Fill in the yellow spaces below with the correct adjective.

new	newer	newest
warm	warmer	warmest
hard	harder	hardest
neat	neater	neatest
smart	smarter	smartest
tall	taller	tallest

Spectrum Language Arts
Grade 1

Chapter 3 Lesson 10
Usage
85

85

Review

You use the words **I** and **me** to talk about yourself.

   I can make eggs.   The blue jay saw **me**.

When you talk about yourself and another person, put them first.

   Grandpa and I play chess.   Give the books to **Chen and me**.

Putting It Together
Read each pair of sentences. Make a check mark ✔ next to the one that is correct.

1. _____ Me have a baby sister.

   ___✔___ I have a baby sister.

2. ___✔___ She gives me sloppy kisses.

   _____ She gives I sloppy kisses.

3. ___✔___ Birdy and I play hide and seek.

   _____ Me and Birdy play hide and seek.

4. _____ She likes to chase I, too.

   ___✔___ She likes to chase me, too.

Spectrum Language Arts
Grade 1

Review: Chapter 3 Lessons 9-10
Usage

86

Review

Some adjectives are used to compare. Add **er** to an adjective to compare two things. Add **est** to compare three or more things.

   Mick's room is neat.
   A.J.'s room is neat**er**.
   Izzy's room is neat**est**.

Fill in the blanks in each set of sentences.

1. Duke is a smart dog.

   Bo is _____smarter_____ than Duke.

   Daisy is the _____smartest_____ of all three dogs.

2. My house is old.

   Lena's house is _____older_____ than mine.

   Olly's house is the _____oldest_____.

3. The yellow fish is small.

   The green fish is _____smaller_____.

   The orange fish is the _____smallest_____.

Spectrum Language Arts
Grade 1

Review: Chapter 3 Lessons 9-10
Usage
87

87

Lesson 3.11 Synonyms

Synonyms are words that mean the same or almost the same thing.

   little, small   choose, pick   dad, father

Match It
Read each word. Find its synonym in the box. Write it in the matching mitten.

jump	sleepy	glad
fast	shout	large

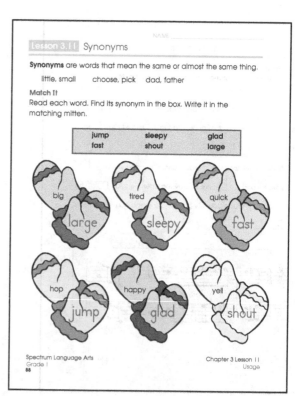

Spectrum Language Arts
Grade 1

Chapter 3 Lesson 11
Usage

88

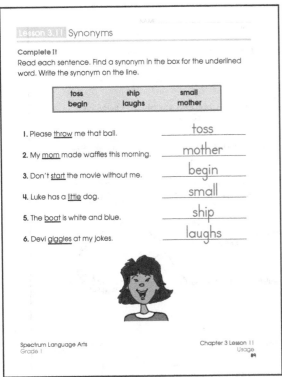

Lesson 3.11 Synonyms

Complete It
Read each sentence. Find a synonym in the box for the underlined word. Write the synonym on the line.

toss	ship	small
begin	laughs	mother

1. Please <u>throw</u> me that ball. toss
2. My <u>mom</u> made waffles this morning. mother
3. Don't <u>start</u> the movie without me. begin
4. Luke has a <u>little</u> dog. small
5. The <u>boat</u> is white and blue. ship
6. Devi <u>giggles</u> at my jokes. laughs

Spectrum Language Arts
Grade 1

Chapter 3 Lesson 11
Usage
89

89

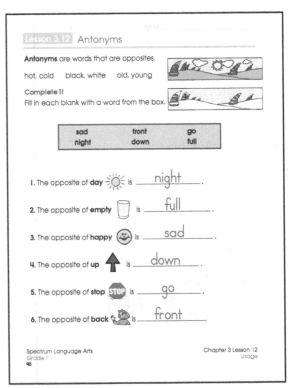

Lesson 3.12 Antonyms

Antonyms are words that are opposites.

hot, cold   black, white   old, young

Complete It
Fill in each blank with a word from the box.

sad	front	go
night	down	full

1. The opposite of **day** is night.
2. The opposite of **empty** is full.
3. The opposite of **happy** is sad.
4. The opposite of **up** is down.
5. The opposite of **stop** is go.
6. The opposite of **back** is front.

Spectrum Language Arts
Grade 1
90

Chapter 3 Lesson 12
Usage

90

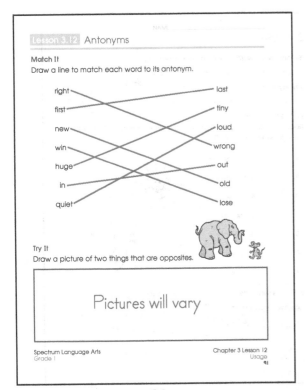

Lesson 3.12 Antonyms

Match It
Draw a line to match each word to its antonym.

right   last
first   tiny
new   loud
win   wrong
huge   out
in   old
quiet   lose

Try It
Draw a picture of two things that are opposites.

Pictures will vary

Spectrum Language Arts
Grade 1

Chapter 3 Lesson 12
Usage
91

91

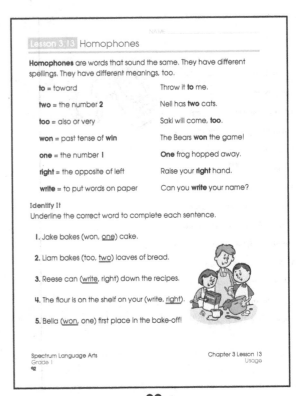

Lesson 3.13 Homophones

Homophones are words that sound the same. They have different spellings. They have different meanings, too.

to = toward	Throw it **to** me.
two = the number **2**	Nell has **two** cats.
too = also or very	Saki will come, **too**.
won = past tense of win	The Bears **won** the game!
one = the number **1**	**One** frog hopped away.
right = the opposite of left	Raise your **right** hand.
write = to put words on paper	Can you **write** your name?

Identify It
Underline the correct word to complete each sentence.

1. Jake bakes (won, <u>one</u>) cake.
2. Liam bakes (too, <u>two</u>) loaves of bread.
3. Reese can (<u>write</u>, right) down the recipes.
4. The flour is on the shelf on your (write, <u>right</u>).
5. Bella (<u>won</u>, one) first place in the bake-off!

Spectrum Language Arts
Grade 1
92

Chapter 3 Lesson 13
Usage

92

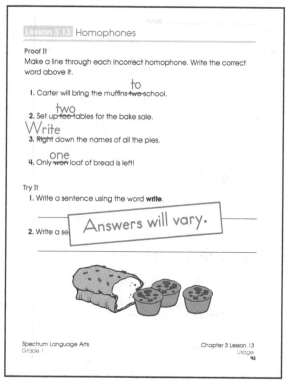

Lesson 3.13 Homophones

Proof It
Make a line through each incorrect homophone. Write the correct word above it.

1. Carter will bring the muffins ~~two~~ *to* school.

2. Set up ~~too~~ *two* tables for the bake sale.

3. ~~Right~~ *Write* down the names of all the pies.

4. Only ~~won~~ *one* loaf of bread is left!

Try It
1. Write a sentence using the word **write**.

2. Write a se
Answers will vary.

Spectrum Language Arts
Grade 1

Chapter 3 Lesson 13
Usage
93

93

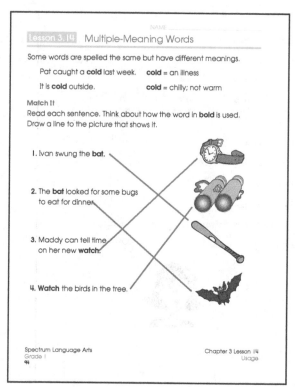

Lesson 3.14 Multiple-Meaning Words

Some words are spelled the same but have different meanings.

Pat caught a **cold** last week. **cold** = an illness

It is **cold** outside. **cold** = chilly; not warm

Match It
Read each sentence. Think about how the word in **bold** is used. Draw a line to the picture that shows it.

1. Ivan swung the **bat**.

2. The **bat** looked for some bugs to eat for dinner.

3. Maddy can tell time on her new **watch**.

4. **Watch** the birds in the tree.

Spectrum Language Arts
Grade 1

Chapter 3 Lesson 14
Usage
94

94

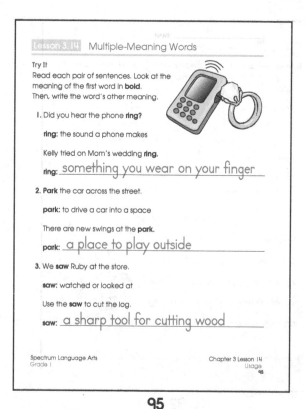

Lesson 3.14 Multiple-Meaning Words

Try It
Read each pair of sentences. Look at the meaning of the first word in **bold**. Then, write the word's other meaning.

1. Did you hear the phone **ring**?

ring: the sound a phone makes

Kelly tried on Mom's wedding **ring**.

ring: *something you wear on your finger*

2. **Park** the car across the street.

park: to drive a car into a space

There are new swings at the **park**.

park: *a place to play outside*

3. We **saw** Ruby at the store.

saw: watched or looked at

Use the **saw** to cut the log.

saw: *a sharp tool for cutting wood*

Spectrum Language Arts
Grade 1

Chapter 3 Lesson 14
Usage
95

95

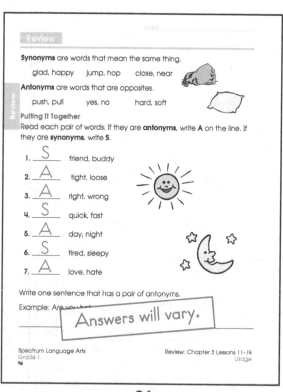

Review

Synonyms are words that mean the same thing.

glad, happy jump, hop close, near

Antonyms are words that are opposites.

push, pull yes, no hard, soft

Putting It Together
Read each pair of words. If they are **antonyms**, write **A** on the line. If they are **synonyms**, write **S**.

1. __S__ friend, buddy
2. __A__ tight, loose
3. __A__ right, wrong
4. __S__ quick, fast
5. __A__ day, night
6. __S__ tired, sleepy
7. __A__ love, hate

Write one sentence that has a pair of antonyms.

Example: Are you h
Answers will vary.

Spectrum Language Arts
Grade 1

Review: Chapter 3 Lessons 11–14
Usage
96

96

Review

Homophones are words that sound the same. They have different spellings. They have different meanings, too.

to = toward   **two** = the number **2**   **too** = also or very

won = past tense of **win**   **one** = the number **1**

right = the opposite of **left**   **write** = to put words on paper

Write the word from the box that completes each sentence.

1. | write   right | Nate turned ___right___ at the stop sign.

2. | Two   Too | ___Two___ kids were at the front of the group.

3. | to   two | Ms. Dugg gave some water ___to___ us.

4. | won   one | Only ___one___ person can come in first.

Spectrum Language Arts
Grade 1

Review: Chapter 3 Lessons 11–14
Usage
97

97